KOGAN
PAGE

Kogan Page
Educational
Management
Series

TOTAL QUALITY MANAGEMENT IN EDUCATION

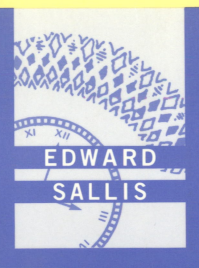

EDWARD SALLIS

TOTAL QUALITY MANAGEMENT IN EDUCATION

Kogan Page

Educational

Management

Series

TOTAL QUALITY MANAGEMENT IN EDUCATION

EDWARD SALLIS

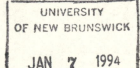

KOGAN
PAGE

Philadelphia • London

For Kate

First published in 1993

Apart from any fair dealing for the purposes of research or private study, or criticism or review, as permitted under the Copyright, Designs and Patents Act, 1988, this publication may only be reproduced, stored or transmitted, in any form or by any means, with the prior permission in writing of the publishers, or in the case of reprographic reproduction in accordance with the terms of licences issued by the Copyright Licensing Agency. Enquiries concerning reproduction outside those terms should be sent to the publishers at the undermentioned address:

Kogan Page Limited
120 Pentonville Road
London N1 9JN

© Edward Sallis, 1993

British Library Cataloguing in Publication Data

A CIP record for this book is available from the British Library.

ISBN 0 7494 0818 9

Typeset by DP Photosetting, Aylesbury, Bucks
Printed and bound in Great Britain by
Biddles Ltd, Guildford and King's Lynn

Contents

Preface and Acknowledgements

One of the most important contemporary challenges facing schools, colleges and universities is how to manage for quality. This book introduces the reader to Total Quality Management (TQM) and discusses its relevance to education. The aim is to provide hard-pressed educational managers with a ready guide to the issues TQM raises and to quality management techniques.

To a few readers some of the content may come as a surprise. A proportion of the book is about quality in general and TQM in industry. This is not because I take the view that business methods are superior to ideas developed from educational practice, or that education will be improved just by adopting the language of commerce. Far from it, and there is much that business can learn from the way that some of our best schools, colleges and universities are run. Simply, space is given to business examples because the origins of TQM are in business, and in particular in manufacturing, and to understand TQM it is necessary to take account of its ancestry. However, what has struck me when researching TQM is how much its philosophy corresponds with the best educational management practice.

I have deliberately used the language of industrial TQM in this book because this has become the technical vocabulary of the subject. I recognize that many practitioners in education do not find it appealing. The use of the term 'customer', especially when discussing pupils and students, can cause a great deal of controversy. There are difficulties with it in education, particularly in relation to ideas such as 'the customers' wishes are always paramount'. If the technical vocabulary is not to your taste simply do not use it. However, a word of warning needs to be sounded. Do not throw the baby out with the bath water. It is easy to lose the concept when the language is changed. Total quality is an idea which has to be communicated and a change of vocabulary may confuse or cause a loss of direction. It also makes it very difficult to hold a dialogue with industry, which is useful as this is where much of the pioneering work has been done. 'Customer' and 'customer satisfaction' are consciously used when discussing TQM to emphasize the service relationship of the institution to those who keep it in work. It is a simple but extremely powerful notion which any organization will be foolish to ignore.

The book's message is that an understanding of quality derived from business experience is applicable to education, but that it requires a degree of adaptation to fit both the general educational setting and the particular circumstances of each school, college or university. Each institution needs to decide its own destiny, but an understanding of how the best organizations in other fields of endeavour do things will not go amiss.

TQM is a means of assuring quality and standards in education. It provides a philosophy as well as a set of tools for improving quality. It is achieved by putting a simple but central idea into operation. The principal idea behind TQM is that customers and their interests should come first: an easily understood idea, but one whose implementation demands a high degree of commitment. There is no single specification for TQM. Different organizations pursue TQM in their own way. Thankfully, TQM is very flexible and can be adapted to meet the particular needs and circumstances of all institutions, large or small. However, no book can tell an institution how to achieve total quality for itself – only your customers can tell you that! This book raises the issues and gives guidance on the main questions that will be raised for any educational institution which decides to travel the TQM route.

The need for a book on TQM in education was highlighted by the response to the *National Quality Survey* (1991) which I carried out in the autumn of 1990. While this was a survey of FE colleges, it demonstrated the degree of interest nationally in TQM and quality issues in general. In the last couple of years awareness has increased. People from all sectors of education are now expressing an interest. Many institutions, regardless of size, are beginning to put the philosophy of TQM into practice. This growth of interest has stimulated a demand for publications which address the issues the subject raises for education. I have already given this some initial consideration in the further education context in *College Quality Assurance Systems* (1991) and *Total Quality Management* (1992), both jointly written with Peter Hingley and published by The Staff College, Coombe Lodge. This book casts its net wider, develops the topic, and considers TQM in the broader educational setting.

Many people have contributed to my thinking about quality matters and TQM in education. My special thanks go to Dr Bill Bevan, Principal of Brunel College of Technology, who originally stimulated my interest in TQM and who has been a constant source of support. Dr Peter Hingley, Reader in Management at the University of the West of England Bristol, has been an inspiration for much of the book. I am fortunate to have Peter's intellectual stimulation and his friendship. Both Sefton Davies of SDA Associates and Dave Pardy of QIMM Development have demonstrated to me the power of training as a developmental tool for quality. Professor Paul Croll, also of The University of the West of England, has put rigour into my thinking, and Dr Gerry Gregory of Brunel University has provided me with a platform to try out ideas. The staff and students of Brunel College of Technology have proved to me that it is people who deliver quality in education. I would also like to thank Callie Zilinsky and Carol Tyler and the staff of the Quality Academy of Fox Valley Technical College, Appleton, Wisconsin for spending time explaining to me their long-standing and pioneering approach to TQM. Without Kate Sallis of Soundwell College the book would have been neither started nor finished. As always it is as much Kate's book as mine.

Total quality management is a collaborative venture and I would like to express my thanks to the following people for their help, support and encouragement: Sue Boyd, Ken Stevens, Peter Walters, and all the very enthusiastic and committed members of the Quality Assurance Steering Group of Brunel College of Technology; Maryl Chambers of Avon County Council; Mike Barrett and Marion Thorpe of East Birmingham College; Margaret Cockburn, Dr David Collins and Dr Iain MacRoberts of Sandwell College of Further and Higher Education; Lynton Gray of The Staff College; Tony Halsall of Afan College; Jimmy Johnston and all the members of the North Bristol TVEI Consortium; Gordon Lyon formerly of the Scottish Office Education Department; John Marsh of Avon TEC; Christine Pickup of North Yorkshire LEA and Norman Woollard of Milton Keynes College and all the members of their National Quality Development Support Network; Joan Boland of Bramston School; Dr Bert Roberts of Eastleigh College; Trevor Holroyd of Ernest Ireland Construction; Robert Mair and Kerr Stirling of Rolls-Royce Military Engines; Roy Stickland formerly of TEED, and now of First Concern; Helen Mahon, Alastair Nielson and Professor Harry Rothman of the Bristol Business School; Howard Green, formerly of Oxford Polytechnic, and now Principal of Eggbuckland Community College, Plymouth; Heather Speller of South Kent College; Lawrence Thirlaway of Mid-Warwickshire College; and Helen Carley and Robert Jones of Kogan Page. Lee Walder of Brunel College of Technology and Georgia Goldner of In-House Publishing, Bath, professionally produced the graphics. Thanks are also due to BSI Quality Assurance for permission to quote from British Standard 5750. In naming people there is always the danger of overlooking someone. Many other people have been of tremendous assistance and inspiration, and if you are one of them, thank you.

Chapter 1

The Background to the Quality Movement

Quality is about passion and pride.
(Tom Peters and Nancy Austin, *A Passion For Excellence*,
1985, p 101)

The message of quality

Quality is at the top of most agendas and improving quality is probably the most important task facing any institution. However, despite its importance many people find quality a most enigmatic concept. It is perplexing to define and even more difficult to measure. One person's idea of quality often conflicts with another's, and as we are all too aware, no two experts ever come to the same conclusion when discussing what makes a good school or college.

Of course, we all know quality when we experience it, but describing and explaining it is a more difficult task. In our everyday life we usually take quality for granted, especially when it is regularly provided. Yet we are all too acutely aware when it is lacking. We often only recognize the importance of quality when we experience the frustration and time-wasting associated with its absence. Of one thing we can be certain. Quality is what makes the difference between things being excellent or run-of-the-mill. Increasingly, in education quality makes the difference between success and failure. This will certainly be the case as grant maintained schools proliferate, sixth-form and FE colleges gain their corporate status and all sectors of education face the full rigours of the new educational market places.

The best organizations, whether public or private, understand quality and know its secret. Seeking the source of quality is an important quest. Education is also recognizing the need to pursue it, and to deliver it to their pupils and students. There are plenty of candidates for the source of quality in education – well-maintained buildings; outstanding teachers; high moral values; excellent examination results; specialization; the support of parents, business and the local community; plentiful resources; the application of the latest technology; strong and purposeful leadership; the care and concern for pupils and students; a well-balanced curriculum, or some combination of these factors.

It may be instructive to look to the business world for an insight into the starting point for our discussion of quality. IBM's definition puts it simply: 'Quality equals customer satisfaction' (Unterberger, 1991, p 3). Alex Trotman, an Executive Vice-President of the Ford Motor Company has delivered the same message: 'We know these days, in these tough times, that we have to satisfy our customers completely' (Artzt et al, 1992, p 17). It is not quite as simple as 'listen and respond to your customers and all the other good things will follow', but it is a serious start. Organizations who take quality seriously know that much of the secret of quality stems from listening to and responding sympathetically to the needs and wants of their customers and clients. Quality involves doing many other things well, but unless an institution puts its customers first the preconditions for developing quality will not exist.

Is quality just another initiative?

Quality is an idea whose time has come. It is on everyone's lips. The Citizen's Charter, The Parent's Charter, Investors in People, The European Quality Award, British Standard BS5750 and International Standard ISO9000 are just some of the quality awards and standards which have been introduced in recent years to promote quality and excellence. This new consciousness of quality has now reached education. British education has long had quality mechanisms in place, although many of them have been external to institutions. HMI and local authority inspectors, and the systems operated by examining and validating bodies, are all important in the pursuit of quality. The difference now is that institutions are being required to develop their own quality systems, and to be able to demonstrate publicly that they can deliver a quality service.

We need to ask whether quality, quality assurance, total quality, and TQM are just more initiatives – other new fads designed to add to the workload of already hard-pressed teachers and underfunded institutions? Initiative fatigue has been a symptom of a hard-pressed education system for the last decade, and the rate of change shows no sign of slowing. Why impose quality on top of all the other innovations which schools, colleges and universities are having to cope with? If quality is just another of those good ideas, hastily thrown up only to be as quickly forgotten, then educators have the right to be sceptical.

Quality, especially in the guise of Total Quality Management (TQM), is different. It is not just another initiative. It is a philosophy and a methodology which assists institutions to manage change, and to set their own agendas for dealing with the plethora of new external pressures. Considerable claims are made for TQM. In the industrial sphere it is seen as the means by which beleaguered economies in the West can transform themselves to compete better with the fast growth economies of the Pacific rim. There are those in education who believe that TQM properly applied to it can complete a similar transformation. However, TQM does not and will not bring results overnight. The essence of TQM is a change of culture. Changing the culture of an institution is a slow process, and one that is best not rushed. If the effects of TQM are to be lasting people have to want to be on board. It is not always comfortable putting the customer first. The quality message must reach people's hearts and minds. In education this will only happen if staff can be convinced that it makes sense for them and benefits their learners.

The industrial origins of the quality movement

The pursuit of quality is not new. There has always been a need to ensure that products conform to their specification and give their customers satisfaction and value for money. Achieving consistent quality allows consumers to have confidence in a product and its producers. The marks of gold- and silversmiths are evidence of this longstanding concern. However, quality became an issue with the advent of industrialization. Prior to this craftsmen set and maintained their own standards on which their reputations and livelihoods depended. It was the breaking down of work into narrow and repetitive tasks with the advent of mass production which took away from the worker the possibility of self-checking quality. The responsibility of the worker for the quality of the product, which is an essential feature of a craft, was lost when goods were mass produced. New production methods, associated with the scientific approach to management and the name of F W Taylor, at the turn of the century, reduced many in the workforce to human components in the process of manufacture. A strict division of labour developed from it and necessitated the expansion of the system of inspection known as quality control.

Quality control and inspection are processes which ensure that only those products which meet their specification leave the factory gate. However, quality control is an after-the-event process, and one divorced from the people who produce the product. Inspection and quality control detect defective products. They are not means of assuring that the workforce cares about quality. They are necessary processes under mass production, but they are often wasteful and expensive, involving considerable amounts of scrap and reworking. Quality control and inspection, by themselves, are increasingly being seen as uneconomic. Many companies are replacing or augmenting them with methods of quality assurance and quality improvement which seek to build quality into production by returning to the workforce their responsibility for quality.

Notions of quality improvement and quality assurance began to emerge after the Second World War. However, in Britain and the USA they only began to attract attention on a large scale in the 1980s as companies started to ask questions about the superiority of the Japanese in capturing an increasing share of world markets. Questions were asked about their success, and whether it is bound up with their national culture and management techniques. To answer the questions about the origin of quality management techniques we need to start the search in the USA in the late 1920s.

The contributions of Deming, Shewhart and Juran

Notions of quality assurance and total quality were late in arriving in the West, although the ideas were originally developed in the 1930s and 1940s by, among others, W Edwards Deming. An American statistician with a PhD in physics, Deming was born in 1900. His influence as a management theorist has only been of recent origin in the West, although the Japanese have been calling on his talents since 1950.

Deming began formulating his ideas in the 1930s while working on methods of removing variability and waste from industrial processes. He started work at Western Electric's legendary Hawthorne plant in Chicago, where Joseph Juran, the other main American contributor to the Japanese quality revolution, was also employed. The Hawthorne plant at the time employed over 40,000 people manufacturing telephone equipment. It was made famous by Elton Mayo and his colleagues from Harvard University, who between 1927 and 1932 carried out their famous series of experiments on the causes of productivity changes. It was there that Mayo and his team discovered the 'Hawthorne effect', and recognized the existence and importance to industrial output and productivity of the informal structures within organizations and their impact on working practices.

From Western Electric Deming moved to work at the US Department of Agriculture. While working there he was introduced to Walter Shewhart, a statistician from the Bell Laboratories in New York. Shewhart had developed techniques to bring industrial processes into what he called statistical control. These are a series of techniques for removing the sources of variability from industrial processes, so enabling them to be made more predictable and controllable. The aim was to eliminate waste and delay. Deming's initial contribution was to develop and advance the statistical methods of Shewhart. The statistical methods of Shewhart and Deming, now known as Statistical Process Control (SPC), combined with the insights of the human relations movement associated with Mayo and his colleagues, are the theoretical underpinnings of TQM.

Deming first visited Japan in the late 1940s to work on their post-war census. Impressed by his work, the Japanese Union of Engineers and Scientists invited him to return in 1950 to lecture to leading Japanese industrialists on the application of statistical process control.

The Japanese were concerned to reconstruct their war-torn industry. Japanese industry had been largely destroyed by American bombing, and what was left mainly produced poor quality imitations of other nations' products. The Japanese wanted to learn the lessons, particularly the quality control lessons, from other industrialized nations.

Deming gave his Japanese audiences a simple answer to their predicament. He told them to start by finding out what their customers wanted. Once they knew that he suggested that they design both their methods of production and their products to the highest standards. This would enable them to take the lead. Deming believed that such an approach, if thoroughly carried out, would take the average company about five years to establish itself as a market leader. The Japanese put into practice the ideas of Deming, Joseph Juran and other American quality experts who visited Japan at the time. The quality revolution started in manufacturing and was followed by service industries and by banking and finance. The Japanese have developed the ideas of Juran and Deming into what they call Total Quality Control (TQC), and have both captured and created a lion's share of many world markets. Much of this market dominance is the result of their concern for quality. Their most famous national writer on quality, Kauro Ishikawa, has described the Japanese approach to TQC as 'a thought revolution in management'. (Ishikawa, 1985, p 1).

The recent growth of interest in quality

In their native USA the ideas of Deming and Juran were ignored. In the 1950s and 60s American businesses could sell everything they made in a world hungry for manufactured goods. The emphasis of American and most Western manufacturing industry was on maximizing output and profit. In the sellers' market which existed at the time for their goods, quality had a low priority. It is only since the late 1970s when they had lost both markets and market share to the Japanese that major US companies have started to take the quality message seriously. They started asking why it was that consumers preferred Japanese products. In the USA, the turning point came in 1980 with a nationwide NBC documentary called 'If Japan Can, Why Can't We?'

The programme highlighted the dominance of Japanese industry in many US markets. The latter part of the programme featured Deming and his contribution to Japanese economic success. Since then the message of Deming and Juran, together with that of other quality experts including Philip B Crosby and Armand V Feigenbaum, has caught the imagination of business both in the USA and in Western Europe, although the reality is that only a minority of companies are seriously implementing TQM. Nevertheless, quality has been put firmly on many agendas, although there is a long way to go before TQM becomes the norm.

The quest for the answer to Japanese competition was highlighted in one of the most influential of management texts of the 1980s: Peters and Waterman, *In Search of Excellence* (1982). Peters and Waterman analysed the essential features of the 'excellent' company based on the best practice then existing in the USA. Their research showed that those companies which have excellent relationships with their customers are often those which are the most competitive and profitable. Excellence goes hand in hand with simple, but crucial notions, of being 'close to the customers' and with an obsession with quality. The excellent organizations have simple and non-bureaucratic structures based on active and enthusiastic teams. These features can be part of any organization whatever its national and cultural origins, but they are ones which many Japanese companies have enthusiastically embraced.

The message of total quality requires managers to put aside short-term preoccupations and take a longer-term view. Staying ahead of the competition requires organizations to seek out their customers' requirements and then to be single-minded in the way they organize to meet and exceed them. It is generally recognized that Japan's place as the world's leading industrial power is based to a considerable extent on taking the quality message to heart by planning long-term and putting the emphasis on designing quality into their products and into their employee attitudes and relationships.

The differences between Japanese business methods and those of Western industry are cultural, but not entirely in the national cultural sense. The major difference is in the culture of their companies and their attitude to quality. All the major 'gurus', Deming, Juran, Crosby and Peters argue the need for a change of work culture if total quality is to succeed. Many examples of excellence abound in the West, and the success of companies like British Airways has been attributed to their embrace of TQM. In Britain and Western Europe the message of quality assurance has only recently been heard, but there is an increasing realization that quality is the key to competitive advantage. Competition is not only for market share, but for employing the most innovative and motivated employees. There is now the drive to enhance Europe-wide quality certification standards post-1992, and The European Foundation for Quality Management has recently been established by 14 major European companies, including Volkswagen, BT, and Philips.

The quality movement in education

The movement for total quality in education is of more recent origin. There are few references in the literature before the late 1980s. Much of the pioneering work of reorganizing work practices on TQM lines has been carried out by a few community colleges in the USA and by some UK further education colleges. The initiatives in the USA developed somewhat before those in Britain, but in both countries the surge of interest occurred from 1990 onwards. Many of the ideas associated with quality are also well developed in higher education and notions of quality are increasingly being investigated and implemented in schools.

While this book does not deal with the teaching of TQM as an academic subject it is interesting to note that despite the growth of interest in it as a means of generating greater productivity it has made little headway as an academic subject. In a recent survey carried out by Robert Kaplan of the Harvard Business School he found only a small input on TQM on most of the MBA and business programmes in 20 leading US universities, as well as a dearth of research effort. A similar state of affairs exists in Europe where there is also a gap between the needs of industry for teaching and research into TQM and the curricula of business programmes. There is as yet little understanding of the importance of total quality to economic well-being (Kaplan 1992).

There has been a traditional reluctance in much of British education to embrace industrial management methodologies and language. That may account for the lateness with which the vision of the quality movement has reached education. Many educationalists have disliked drawing analogies between educational processes and the manufacture of industrial products. However, recent initiatives such as TVEI, teacher placements in industry and the growth of Education Business Partnerships have brought education and business closer together and have made industrial concepts more acceptable. There is an increasing willingness by educationalists to explore lessons from industry.

The upsurge of interest in education coincided, in the UK, with the passing of the Education Reform Act in 1988. The Act placed considerable emphasis on the monitoring of the educational process through performance indicators. However, performance indicators are mainly a guide to the efficiency of the process. They provide only rudimentary measures of the quality of learning, or of the effectiveness of the institution in meeting its customers' needs. Institutions which have wanted to go beyond performance indicators have started to look seriously at TQM as a means of improving their standards of service.

Quality improvement becomes increasingly important as institutions achieve greater control over their own affairs. Greater freedom has to be matched by greater accountability. Institutions have to demonstrate that they are able to offer a quality education to their learners. We live in an era of greater competition where many of the old certainties are disappearing. We now find schools being encouraged to offer vocational education – the traditional market of FE colleges. National Vocational Qualifications, once the sole province of the FE colleges, are being increasingly offered directly by employers, a move which may be hastened by the introduction of training credits. Hosts of other changes are taking place in the educational landscape including the extension of higher education courses being franchised to FE colleges. Higher education is being funded to increase student numbers with reduced unit costs. League tables provide parents with better information on which to make comparisons and choices in the era of open enrolment. The introduction of training credits is designed to put the power of choice into the hands of the 16+ consumer. Grant-maintained schools and corporate sixth-form and FE colleges have spelt the end of local authority post-16 strategic planning, and the 1992 White Paper *Choice and Diversity* will severely restrict, if not remove entirely, the role of local government in education. This deregulation of educational provision requires competitive strategies which clearly differentiate institutions from their competitors. Quality may sometimes be the only differentiating factor for an institution.

Focusing on the needs of the customer, which is at the heart of quality, is one of the most effective means of facing the competition and surviving.

The concept of TQM has received official sanction, at least in post-16 education. The White Paper *Education and Training for the 21st Century*, which preceded the 1992 Further and Higher Education Act, contains the expectation that the newly incorporated FE and sixth-form colleges will each have a system of quality assurance. TQM is among the systems mentioned. In higher education the Committee of Vice-Chancellors and Principals published *Teaching Standards and Excellence in Higher Education* in 1991, which was sub-titled *Developing a Culture for Quality*. In its conclusion its authors propose that 'Each university should establish its own tailored Total Quality Management system' (Elton and Partington, 1991, p 13). What is so surprising is why quality and total quality have taken so long to achieve prominence in education. However, of one thing we can be certain, assuring the quality of service is a key issue for all sectors of education for the next decade.

Chapter 2

Understanding the Concept of Quality

Soon the thought interrupted again. *Quality?* There was something irritating, even angering about that question. He thought about it, and then thought about it some more, and then looked out of the window, and then thought about it some more. *Quality? ...* It wasn't until three in the morning that he wearily confessed to himself that he didn't have a clue as to what Quality was, picked up his briefcase and headed home ... and when he woke up the next morning there was Quality staring him in the face.
(Robert M Pirsig, *Zen And The Art Of Motorcycle Maintenance*, 1974, p 186)

The concept of quality

Quality has a variety of contradictory meanings. As Naomi Pfeffer and Anna Coote have observed in their discussion of quality in the welfare services 'Quality is a slippery concept' (Pfeffer and Coote, 1991, p 31). It implies different things to different people. Everyone is in favour of providing quality education. The arguments start because there is a lack of agreement as to what it means. It is, therefore, necessary to have a clear understanding of the various meanings of quality otherwise there is a danger that it becomes a mere catchphrase, a word with high moral tone but little practical value. An understanding of the diverse meanings of quality is a necessary starting point for our discussion of TQM.

A possible reason for the enigmatic nature of quality is that it is a dynamic idea. The emotional and moral force which quality possesses makes it a difficult idea to tie down. There is the danger that much of its vitality can be lost if it is subjected to too much academic analysis. Westley and Mintzberg make the point that this happens to many important concepts which are freely used in practical settings:

A strange process seems to occur as concepts such as culture and charisma [and we can add quality] move from practice to academic research. Loosely used in practice, these concepts, as they enter academia become subjected to a concerted effort to force them to lie down and behave, to render them properly scientific. In the process they seem to lose emotional resonance, no longer expressing the reality that practitioners originally tried to capture (Westley and Mintzberg, 1991, p 40).

Quality is a dynamic idea and exact definitions are not particularly helpful. However, its range of meanings does cause confusion. Important practical consequences flow from these different meanings. For this reason they need discussion.

Quality as an absolute concept

Some of the confusion over the meaning of quality arises because it can be used both as an absolute and a relative concept. Quality in everyday conversation is mainly used as an absolute. People use it to describe expensive restaurants and luxury cars. As an absolute, quality is similar in nature to goodness, beauty, and truth; an ideal with which there can be no compromise. In the absolute definition things which exhibit quality are of the highest possible standard which cannot be surpassed. Quality products are things of perfection made with no expense spared. They are valuable and convey prestige to their owners. 'Quality cars', for example, are hand-built and expensive and have interiors of walnut and leather. Rarity and expense are two of the features of quality in this definition. Quality in this sense is used to convey status and positional advantage, and the ownership of things of 'quality' sets their owners apart from those who cannot afford them. It is synonymous with 'high quality or top quality'. To use the words of Pfeffer and Coote again, 'Most of us admire it, many of us want it, few of us can have it' (Pfeffer and Coote, 1991, p 4). Used in the educational context this concept of quality is essentially elitist. By definition only a few institutions are able to offer such a 'high quality' educational experience to their learners. Most learners cannot afford it, and most institutions cannot aspire to provide it.

The absolute notions of 'high quality' have little to do with TQM. However, the absolute meaning often sticks in discussions of TQM. So even when addressing quality in its technical, TQM, sense there is still an aura of luxury and status about it. Quality has class. This subtle and often subliminal use of language can be useful for public relations purposes, and may help an educational institution promote ideas of quality. It also demonstrates that pursuing quality is all about performing to the highest standards.

The relative concept of quality

Quality can also be employed as a relative concept. This is the sense in which it is used in TQM. The relative definition views quality not as an attribute of a product or service, but as something which is ascribed to it. Quality can be judged to exist when a good or service meets the specification that has been laid down for it. Quality is not the end in itself, but a means by which the end product is judged to be up to standard. Quality products or services, in this relative or ascribed definition need not be expensive and exclusive. They may be beautiful, but not necessarily so. They do not have to be special. They can be ordinary, commonplace, and familiar. Overhead projectors, ballpoint pens, and the school catering service may all exhibit quality if they meet simple but crucially important standards. They must do what they claim to do, and do what their customers expect of them. In other words they must be 'fit for their purpose,' as the British Standards Institution defines quality.

The relative definition of quality has two aspects to it. The first is measuring up to specification. The second is meeting customer requirements. The first usage – measuring up – is often summed up as 'fitness for purpose or use'. This is sometimes called the producer definition of quality. Quality for the producer is achieved by its products or services meeting a pre-defined specification in a consistent fashion. Quality is demonstrated by a producer having a system, known as a quality assurance system, which enables the consistent production of the good or service to a particular standard or specification. A product exhibits quality so long as it consistently meets its maker's claims for it.

In this definition both Rover cars and Rolls-Royces are quality products. Luxury, beauty, exclusivity and price do not enter into the equation. So long as products conform to their manufacturers' specifications and standards they exhibit quality. This view of quality is sometimes called 'quality in fact'. 'Quality in fact' is the basis of the quality assurance systems devised in accordance with the British Standards Institution in the BS5750 standard or the identical international standard ISO9000. These standards are fully described in Chapter 5.

The consumer definition of quality

Who should decide whether a school or college is providing a quality service? The answer will tell us much about the values and aspirations of the institution. It is essential to have a clear idea of who is ascribing the attribute of quality: is it the producer or the consumer? The reason for posing this question is because the views of producers and consumers are not always identical. It does happen that perfectly good and useful products and services are rejected by consumers. Making a product to specification does not guarantee sales. A different version of the ascribed view of quality is needed to take account of this problem.

Organizations who follow the TQM path regard quality as being defined by their customers. The reason for this is simple. Customers are the final arbitrators of quality and without them the institution does not exist. The TQM institution has to use all means at its disposal to explore its customers' requirements. As Edwin L. Artzt, Chairman and Chief Executive of the Proctor and Gamble Company, has put it: 'Our customers are both those who retail our products and those who ultimately use them. Total quality means knowing them in ways and depths never fully explored before and using this knowledge to translate needs into innovative new products and business approaches' (Artzt, 1992, p 3).

Quality can be defined as that which best satisfies and exceeds customers needs and wants. This is sometimes called 'quality in perception'. Quality can be said to lie in the eyes of the beholder. This is a very important and powerful definition, and one that any institution ignores at its peril. It is the consumers who make the judgement on quality, which they do by reference to the best comparable performer.

Tom Peters, discussing the pivotal role of the consumer in quality in *Thriving On Chaos*, argues that the *perceived* quality of a business's product or service is the most important single factor affecting its performance. Peters argues that quality as defined by the customer is more important than price in determining the demand for a majority of goods and services. His unequivocal findings are that customers will always pay more for the best quality, regardless of the type of product. He has also found that employees become energized when they have the opportunity to provide a quality service or produce a quality product. However, he does sound a warning because new entrants to the market will also be redefining quality to the customer (see Peters, 1987, p 68).

Figure 2.1 *Quality standards*

PRODUCT & SERVICE STANDARDS

Conformance to Specification

Fitness for Purpose or Use

Zero Defects

Right First Time, Every Time

CUSTOMER STANDARDS

Consumer Satisfaction

Exceeding Customer Expectations

Delighting the Customer

Quality control, quality assurance, and total quality

As well as providing a definition of quality it is necessary to understand the difference between three other important quality ideas. These are the distinctions which are made between quality control, quality assurance and total quality.

Quality control is historically the oldest quality concept. It involves the detection and elimination of components or final products which are not up to standard. It is an after-the-event process concerned with detecting and rejecting defective items. As a method of ensuring quality it may involve a considerable amount of waste, scrap and reworking. Quality control is usually carried out by quality professionals known as quality controllers or inspectors. Inspection and testing are the most common methods of quality control, and are widely used in education to determine whether standards are being met.

Quality assurance is different from quality control. It is a before and during-the-event process. Its concern is to prevent faults occurring in the first place. Quality is designed into the process to attempt to ensure that the product is produced to a predetermined specification. Simply, quality assurance is a means of producing defect- and fault-free products. The aim, in the words of Philip B Crosby, is 'zero defects'. Quality assurance is about consistently meeting product specification or getting things 'right first time, every time'. Quality assurance is made the responsibility of the workforce, usually working in cells or teams, rather than the inspector, although inspection can have a role to play in quality assurance. The quality of the good or service is assured by there being a system in place, known as a quality assurance system, which lays down exactly how production should take place and to what standards. Quality standards are maintained by following the procedures laid down in the QA system.

Total quality management incorporates quality assurance, and extends and develops it. TQM is about creating a quality culture where the aim of every member of staff is to delight their customers, and where the structure of their organization allows them to do so. In the total quality definition of quality the customer is sovereign. It is the approach popularized by Peters and Waterman in *In Search of Excellence* (1982), and which has been a constant theme of Tom Peters' writings since. Many companies, such as Marks and Spencer,

British Airways, and Sainsburys have been pursuing this approach for a number of years. It is about providing the customer with what they want, when they want it and how they want it. It involves moving with changing customer expectations and fashions to design products and services which meet and exceed their expectations. Only by delighting customers will they return and tell their friends about it (this is sometimes called the 'sell-on' definition of quality). The perceptions and expectations of customers are recognized as being short-term and fickle, and so organizations have to find ways of keeping close to their customers to be able to respond to their changing tastes, needs and wants.

The 'product' of education

It is always necessary to ask two fundamental questions when trying to understand quality in any situation. The first is, what is the product?

Figure 2.2 *The hierarchy of quality concepts*

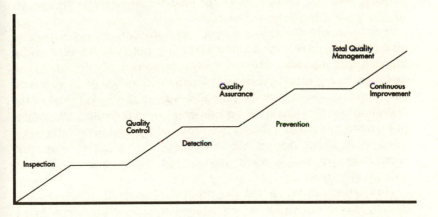

and the second is, who are the customers? These questions are equally applicable to the discussion of quality in education.

What is the product of education? There are a number of different candidates for this title. The pupil or the student is often spoken about as if they are the product. In education we often talk as though learners are the output, especially with reference to the institution's perceived performance over discipline and behaviour. Terms like 'the supply of graduates' make education sound like a production line with students emerging from the end of it. The problem with this definition is that it is difficult to square it with much educational practice.

For a product to be the subject of a quality assurance process the producer needs firstly to specify and control the source of supply. Secondly, the 'raw material' must pass through a standard process or set of processes, and the output must meet predetermined and defined specifications. Such a model does not easily fit education, although there are those that might wish that it would. Such a model would clearly require an initial selection of learners to be made. Some sectors of education do this, but many, following the comprehensive principle of open access, do not. However, it is from there on that the analogy begins to fall apart. While processes such as the national curriculum and the specification of standards and competencies in NVQs have improved the standardization of the process, nevertheless the process of education is anything but uniform.

It is impossible to produce pupils and students to any particular guaranteed standard. As Lynton Gray has put it in his very useful discussion of the issue: 'Human beings are notoriously non-standard, and they bring into educational situations a range of experiences, emotions and opinions which cannot be kept in the background of the operation. Judging quality is very different from inspecting the output of a factory, or judging the service provided by a retail outlet' (Gray, 1992, p 2). The idea of the learner as the product misses the complexities of the learning process and the uniqueness of each individual learner.

How, then, do we define the product? Rather than answer this directly it is more helpful to view education as a service rather than a production line. The distinction between a product and a service is important because there are fundamental differences between them which have a bearing on how their quality can be assured.

Service quality

Service quality characteristics are more difficult to define than those for physical products. This is because they include many important subjective elements. The causes of poor quality and quality failure are different for services and products. Products often fail because of faults in raw materials and components. Their design may be faulty or they may not be manufactured to specification. Poor quality services, on the other hand, are usually directly attributable to employee behaviour or attitude. They often result from lack of care or courtesy. Indifference, lack of training or concern are often principal reasons for a breakdown of service. The different nature of service quality characteristics needs to be borne in mind when discussing educational quality.

Services differ from production in a number of important ways. There are major differences between delivering a service and manufacturing goods. The first difference between the two is that services usually involve direct contact between the provider and the end-users. Services are delivered directly by people to people. There is a close relationship between the customer and the person who delivers the service. The service cannot be separated from the person delivering it or from the person receiving it. Every interaction is different, and the quality of the interaction is in part determined by the customer. The quality of the service is determined both by the person delivering and the person receiving the service. Unlike production there can be no absolute consistency or homogeneity in service delivery. The consistency of the service can only be within boundaries.

Time is the second important element of service quality. Services have to be delivered on time, and this is as important as their physical specification. Additionally, as a service is consumed at the moment of delivery the control of its quality by inspection is always too late. The close personal interactions found in services allow multiple opportunities for feedback and evaluation and these provide the main, but not the only, means of judging whether customers are satisfied with it.

The third difference is that unlike a product, a service cannot be serviced or mended. A poor meal is a poor meal. It cannot be repaired. For this reason it is important that the standard for services should be right first time every time. Paradoxically, it is the high possibility of human error and failing that makes it difficult, if not impossible, to achieve the right first time standard. Nevertheless, this should always be the aim.

Fourth, services face the problem of intangibility. It is often difficult to describe to potential customers exactly what is being offered. It is equally difficult on occasions for customers to describe what they want from the service. Services are largely about process rather than product. It is usually more important how an outcome is arrived at than what the outcome is.

The fact that services are usually rendered directly to customers by junior employees is the fifth distinguishing feature of a service. Senior staff are generally remote from customers. Most customers never have access to senior managers. The quality of the initial interactions colours the view customers have of the whole organization, and so the organization has to find ways of motivating front-line employees to always deliver of their best. This is why training and staff development are of crucial importance. While senior managers may not serve at the front in service organizations they must lead from the front and convey to their staff their vision of the service and the standards they want set for it.

Lastly, it is very difficult to measure successful output and productivity in services. The only meaningful performance indicators are those of customer satisfaction. Intangibles or 'soft' measures are often as important to success and to the customer as are hard and objective performance indicators. 'Soft' indicators – care, courtesy, concern, friendliness, and helpfulness – are often uppermost in customers' minds. Intangibility makes it very difficult to turn round poor service, because it is sometimes impossible to convince dissatisfied customers that a service has changed for the better. Consumers judge quality by comparing their perceptions of what they receive with their expectations of it. Much of this is also true for education. Reputation is crucial to an institutions' success, but the origin of that reputation often defies analysis and measurement. What we do know is that reputation has a great deal to do with the care and concern shown to pupils and students.

For the purposes of analysing quality it is more appropriate to view education as a service industry than as a production process. Once this view is established the institution needs to define clearly the services it is providing and the standards to which they will be delivered. This needs to be carried out in conjunction with all its customer groups, including discussions with governors, parents, and with industry directly or via local Education Business Partnerships.

Education and its customers

We have defined education as a provider of services. Those services include tuition, assessment, and guidance to pupils and students, their parents and sponsors. The customers – the stakeholders of the service – are a very diverse group and need identifying. If quality is about meeting and exceeding customer needs and wants it is important to be clear whose needs and wants we should be satisfying.

It is at this point important to say something about the idea of a 'customer' in the context of education. To some educationalists 'customer' has a distinctly commercial tone which is not applicable to education. They prefer to use client instead. Client, with its connotations of professional service is seen as more appropriate. Stakeholder is another term often used in this context. Others reject all such language and would rather stay with pupil or student. Language is important if an idea is to be acceptable. In this book customer and learner are mainly employed, but there is no quarrel with those who might wish to substitute other terms.

There are others who would make a distinction between 'clients', who are the primary beneficiaries of the education service, and 'customers', who are those who pay for it but who may be at one remove, such as parents, governors, employers or government. In this book customers will be used for both sets of relationships and the distinction will be made between 'primary customers' who directly receive the service, 'secondary customers' such as parents, governors, sponsoring employers of FE students who have a direct stake in the education of a particular individual or in a particular institution, and 'tertiary customers' who have a less direct but none the less crucial stakeholding in education such as future employers, government and society as a whole. To some extent this distinction is at odds with schools' legislation. The 1988 Education Reform Act makes the parents the primary customers of the process. This provides an additional, but not irreconcilable, difficulty for schools. The diversity of customers makes it all the more important for educational institutions to focus on customer wants and to develop mechanisms for responding to them. It is important to define clearly the nature of the service an institution provides to its customers. It is equally important to maintain an excellent and continuing dialogue with them. The best form of marketing is that which the learners do on its behalf. Their successes are also the institution's.

Internal educational customers

A distinction also needs to be made, which will be amplified in Chapter 3, between the external and internal customers of the institution. While the major focus of any school, college or university must be on its external customers – learners, parents, etc – it is important to remember that everyone working in an institution provides services to their colleagues. In TQM staff members are known as internal customers. Poor internal relationships prevent an institution working properly, and in the end it is the external customers who suffer. One of the aims of TQM is to so change the

Figure 2.3   *The customers of education*

Education (Value Added To Learners)	=	The Service
The Learner	=	Primary External Customer or Client
Parents/ Governors/ Employers	=	Secondary External Customer
Labour Market/ Government/ Society	=	Tertiary External Customer
Teachers/ Support Staff	=	Internal Customers

institution that it operates, without internal conflict and competition, as a genuine team with the single objective of satisfying customers.

Reconciling different customer needs

The needs and views of the various customer groups, whether they are internal or external, do not always coincide, especially in large and complex institutions, although the conflict can equally be present in small ones. Potential and actual conflicts of interest will always exist. One of the best methods of resolving different interests is to recognize their existence and to look for the core of issues which unite parties. All stakeholders need to have their views listened to and to be treated fairly. Quality and justice go hand in hand. This is particularly the case when dealing with complaints, which are instances of those 'critical incidents' where it is possible to judge how committed an institution is to a customer-first approach.

It is often difficult to ensure that the learners' views are paramount. There are strong forces pulling against it, not least those that can be exerted by funding processes and mechanisms. Where the needs of the learner and funding mechanisms collide, it is very difficult for an institution to put its learners first. This is particularly the case where funding mechanisms emphasize efficiency which may only be achieved at the cost of quality, eg a staffing cut which leads to a higher pupil–teacher ratio; or where quality assessment in the funding process may not accord with the views on quality which the customers are feeding back. This is a very difficult issue to resolve and TQM does not provide ready answers to it. What it does is to ensure that the institution's processes keep the learners' views centre stage in the strategic planning process. The TQM approach ensures that the institution is conscious of the issues if it is not to trade learners' needs for funding.

The primary focus of any educational institution should be the needs and views of its learners. This does not mean that the views of other stakeholder groups should be ignored. Their views count. However, the learners are the reason why the institution exists and they carry its reputation.

Chapter 3

Total Quality Management in the Educational Context

> TQM is a philosophy of continuous improvement, which can provide any educational institution with a set of practical tools for meeting and exceeding present and future customers needs, wants, and expectations.
> (Edward Sallis)

In previous chapters general ideas of quality have been explored. We need now to see how these can come together in Total Quality Management and to explain its salient features for any school, college or university contemplating its introduction. This chapter explains the key ideas behind TQM in education as well as exploring some of the myths about it.

TQM – some of the misconceptions

Before defining the elements of TQM it may be useful to say a few words about what TQM is not. TQM is not an imposition. It cannot be done to you or for you. For TQM to work an institution must itself want to introduce it. It is not inspection. It is about always trying to do things right first time and every time, rather than occasionally checking if they have gone wrong. TQM is not about working to someone else's agenda, unless the agenda has been specified by your customers and clients. It is not something which only senior managers do and then pass their directions down the line. The 'total' in TQM dictates that everything and everybody in the organization is involved in the enterprise of continuous improvement. The 'management' in TQM likewise means everyone, because everyone in the institution, whatever their status, position or role, is the manager of their own responsibilities. This is a difficult idea to put across, and it is the reason why some organizations talk, as Rolls-Royce do, about Total Quality rather than TQM.

TQM programmes do not have to use the initials TQM. Many organizations pursue the philosophy under their own brand name. Boots the Chemist calls its extensive quality programme 'Assured Shopping'. American Express use the initials AEQL, which stands for American Express Quality Leadership. They prefer to emphasize 'leadership' rather than management (see Artzt et al, 1992, p 16). Total Quality Control, Total Quality Service, Continuous Improvement, Strategic Quality Management, Systematic Improvement, Quality First, Quality Initiatives, Service Quality are some of the many titles used to describe what in this book is called TQM. If a school, for example, felt that it wanted to call its initiative 'Pupils First' or 'The School Improvement Programme' then it should feel free to do so. It is not the name which is important, but the effect which the quality programme will have on the culture of the school. The pupils and their parents will be interested in the change it brings.

TQM is used to describe two slightly different but related notions. The first is a philosophy of continuous improvement. The second related meaning uses TQM to describe the tools and techniques, such as brainstorming and force-field analysis described in Chapter 10, which are used to put quality improvement into action. TQM is both a mind-set and a set of practical activities – an attitude of mind as well as a method of promoting continuous improvement.

Continuous improvement

TQM is a practical but strategic approach to running an organization which focuses on the needs of its customers and clients. It aims to reject any outcome other than excellence. TQM is not a set of slogans, but a deliberate and systematic approach to achieving appropriate levels of quality in a consistent fashion which meet or exceed the needs and wants of customers. It can be thought of as a philosophy of never-ending improvement only achievable by and through people.

As an approach, TQM seeks a permanent shift in an institution's focus away from short-term expediency to the long-term quality improvement. Constant innovation, improvement and change are stressed, and those institutions which practise it lock into a cycle of continuous improvement. They make a conscious attempt to analyse what they are doing and plan to improve it. To create a continuous improvement culture managers have to trust their staff and to delegate decisions to the appropriate level to give staff the responsibility to deliver quality within their own sphere. Staff need the freedom to operate within a framework of clear and known corporate goals.

'Kaizen'

TQM is accomplished by a series of small-scale incremental projects. The Japanese have a word for this approach to continuous improvement: *kaizen*. This is most easily translated as step-by-step improvement. The philosophy of TQM is large-scale, inspirational and all-embracing, but its practical implementation is small-scale, highly practical and incremental. Drastic intervention is not the means of change in TQM. Grandiose schemes are not the way forward, because often they founder for lack of resources, and their demise can breed cynicism and discontent.

The essence of *kaizen* is small projects which seek to build success and confidence, and develop a base for further ventures in improvement. By way of illustration Joseph Juran talks of 'elephant-sized' and 'bite-sized' projects. He argues that the best way to tackle the 'elephant-sized' projects is to divide them up into manageable 'bite-sized' assignments. He recommends assigning one team the task of 'cutting-up the elephant' (Juran, 1989, p 54). Solid and lasting change is based on a long series of small and achievable projects. It is necessary to work through the activities of the institution very carefully, process by process, issue by issue. Over a period of time more is achieved this way than by trying to make large-scale changes. The incremental approach to quality improvement means that implementation need not be an expensive process. Spending money by itself does not produce quality, although when it is carefully targeted it helps.

A change of culture

TQM requires a change of culture. This is notoriously difficult to bring about and takes time to implement. It requires a change of attitudes and working methods. The staff in institutions need to understand and live the message if TQM is to make an impact. However, culture change is not only about changing the behaviour of staff. It also requires a change in the way in which institutions are managed and led. The latter is characterized by an understanding that people, produce quality. Two things are required for staff to produce quality. First, staff need a suitable environment in which to work. They need the tools of the trade and they need to work with systems and procedures which are simple and which aid them in doing their jobs. The environment that surrounds staff has a profound effect on their ability do their job properly and effectively. Among the important environmental features are the systems and procedures with which they work. Laying down good and workable procedures by itself does not produce quality, but if procedures are poor or misleading it makes producing quality extremely difficult. Second, to do a good job staff need encouragement and recognition of their successes and achievements. They need leaders who can appreciate their achievements and coach them to greater success. The motivation to do a good job comes from a leadership style and an atmosphere which heightens self-esteem and empowers the individual.

The upside-down organization

The key to a successful TQM culture is an effective internal/external customer–supplier chain. Once the concept has been grasped it has enormous implications for the organization and the relationships within it. The first casualty is the traditional notion of organizational status. The role of senior and middle management in a TQM culture is to support and empower the teaching and support staff and the learners, not to control them. This can most graphically be illustrated by a comparison of the traditional hierarchical organizational chart with its TQM counterpart. The inverted hierarchy is adapted from the ideas of Karl Albretcht. It seeks to illustrate the paradigm shift implicit in TQM. In education it changes the usual set of relationships to one with a clear customer focus. The upside-down organizational focus does not affect the structure of authority in the school or college, and neither does it diminish the essential leadership role of senior managers. In fact, leadership is pivotal to the success of TQM. The inverted hierarchy emphasizes service-giving relationships and the importance of the customer to the institution.

Figure 3.1 *The hierarchical institution and the upside-down institution in education*

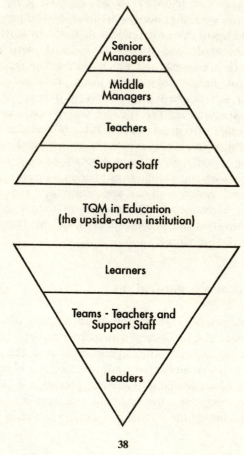

Keeping close to the customers

The primary mission of a TQM institution is to meet the needs and wants of its customers. Excellent organizations, both public and private, keep 'close to the customer', in the words of Peters and Waterman, and have an obsession with quality. They recognize that growth and long-term survival come from matching their service to customer needs. Quality must be matched to the expectations and requirements of customers and clients. Quality is what the customer wants and not what the institution decides is best for them. Without customers there is no institution.

A customer focus is, however, not by itself a sufficient condition for ensuring total quality. TQM organizations need fully worked out strategies for meeting their customers' requirements. Education faces a considerable challenge in its relationships with its external customers. Many customers are often initially uninformed both about the service and what constitutes its quality. Additionally, expectations are diverse and often contradictory. The quality of particular programmes is often confused in the public mind with the reputation of the institution. Learners' perceptions of quality change as they progress through the institution and their experience and confidence grows.

A further difficulty is that education's customers play an important role in the quality of their own learning. The customers have a unique function in determining the quality of what they receive from education. There are difficulties with notions of consistency in the interactive process of learning. To overcome some of these problems it is necessary to ensure the motivation of both the learners and the staff who serve them. It is also important to making clear what is being offered and what is expected of learners.

Colleagues as customers

The customer focus aspect of TQM does not just involve meeting the requirements of the external customers. Colleagues within the institution are also customers, and rely upon internal services of others to do their job effectively. Everyone working in a school, college or university is both a supplier of services and a customer of others. Each member of staff both gives and receives services. Internal customer relationships are vitally important if an institution is to function efficiently and effectively. The best way of developing the internal customer focus is to help individual members of staff to identify the people to whom they provide services. This is known as the 'next-in-line analysis' and revolves round the following questions:

- Whom do you primarily provide a service to?
- Who relies upon what you do to do their job properly?

The people next-in-line are your direct customers, whether they are external to the institution or internal to it. It is important to find out what they want and to have a good idea of the standards they require. The standards may be contractual, but they may also be negotiable. Notions of status and hierarchy do not enter into this relationship. The standard of service provided to someone junior in the institution is as important as the service provided to the Headteacher, the Principal, or the Chair of Governors.

Internal marketing

It is staff who make the quality difference. They produce successful courses and satisfied clients. Internal marketing is a useful tool for communicating with staff to ensure they are kept informed about what is happening in the institution and have the opportunity to feed back ideas. Simply, the idea of internal marketing is that new ideas, products and services have to be as effectively marketed to staff as they are to clients. Staff cannot convey the message of the institution to potential customers without proper product knowledge and an enthusiasm for the institution's aims. Internal marketing is a stage on from communicating ideas. It is a positive and proactive process which demands a commitment to keep staff informed and to listen to their comments.

Professionalism and the customer focus

There is also the additional dimension of a professional workforce in education who have traditionally seen themselves as the guardians of quality and standards. TQM's emphasis on the sovereignty of the customer may cause some conflict with traditional professional concepts. This a difficult area, and one that will need to be considered by any educational institution taking a total quality route. Training for teachers in quality concepts and thinking is an important element in the required culture change. Staff need to understand how they and their pupils and students will benefit from a change to a customer focus. Total quality is about more than being 'nice to customers and smiling'. It is about listening and entering into a dialogue about peoples' fears and aspirations. The best aspects of the professional role are about care and high academic and vocational standards. Blending the best aspects of professionalism with total quality is essential to success.

The quality of learning

Education is about people learning. If TQM is to have relevance in education it needs to address the quality of the learners' experience. Unless it does that it will not make a substantial contribution to quality in education. In a period when most institutions are being asked to do more with less it is important that they focus on their prime activity – learning.

Learners are all different and learn best in a style suited to their needs and inclinations. An educational institution which takes the total quality route must take seriously the issue of learning styles and needs to have strategies for individualization and differentiation in learning. The learner is the primary customer, and unless the learning style meets individual requirements it will not be possible for that institution to claim that it has achieved total quality.

Educational institutions have an obligation to make learners aware of the variety of learning methods available to them. They need to give learners opportunities to sample learning in a variety of different styles. Institutions need to understand that many learners also like to switch and mix-'n'-match styles and must try to be sufficiently flexible to provide choice in learning. Miller, Dower, and Inniss make the same point in *Improving Quality in Further Education*. Their argument, which applies to any other type of institution, is that the FE college should 'ensure that learners experience a range of teaching and learning styles so that their chance of success is maximised' (Miller, Dower, and Inniss, 1992, p 20).

Much work has still to be done on how to use TQM principles in the classroom. Some of the elements might involve the following pattern. A start could be made with the learners and their teachers establishing their 'mission', which could take the form of 'All Shall Succeed'. From this, negotiation might take place about how the two parties will seek to achieve the mission – the styles of learning and teaching and the resources they require. Individual learners may negotiate their own action plans to give them motivation and direction. The process of negotiation may require the establishment of a quality steering committee or forum to provide feedback and to give the learners an opportunity to manage their own learning. Parents or employers might well be represented on it. Detailed monitoring through progress charting will need to be undertaken by both teachers and students to ensure that all are on track. This is important to ensure that timely and appropriate corrective action can be applied if there is a danger of failure.

The establishing of a strong feedback loop is an important element of any quality assurance process. Evaluation should be a continuous process and not just left until the end of the programme of study. The results of evaluation processes should be discussed with the students, perhaps by means of completing a record of achievement. The very act of being involved in evaluation will assist in building up the students' analytical skills.

It is important that the institution uses the results of the formal monitoring to establish the validity of its programmes. It must be prepared to take the necessary corrective action if the customers' experiences do not meet their expectations. None of this is easy as teachers who have pioneered such processes know. It can be an emotional experience and one that can take unexpected turns. What it does is to provide students with motivation and the practical experience of the use of TQM tools which are transferable to other situations.

Barriers to be overcome when introducing TQM

TQM is hard work. It takes time to develop a quality culture. By themselves hard work and time are two of the most formidable blocking mechanisms to quality improvement. TQM needs a champion in the face of the myriad of new challenges and changes facing education. Quality improvement is a fragile process. All major changes are. Cultures are essentially conservative and homeostasis is the norm. Most staff are most comfortable with what they know and understand. However, to stand still while competitors are improving is a recipe for failure.

(If TQM is to work it must have the long-term devotion of the senior staff of the institution. They must back it and drive it. Senior management may themselves be the problem. They may want the results which TQM can bring, but be unwilling to give it their wholehearted support. / Many quality initiatives falter because senior managers quickly return to traditional ways of managing. Fear by senior managers of adopting new methods and approaches is a major barrier. This is potentially the most serious of blockages. If senior management do not give TQM their backing there is little that anyone else in the organization can do.

The sheer volume of external pressures also stands in the way of many organizations attempting TQM. Although quality programmes are introduced with considerable publicity, too often they can be overtaken and submerged by other initiatives. There is a need to ensure that despite other pressures quality always has an important place on the agenda. This is where strategic planning plays such an important role. If TQM is firmly a part of the strategic role of the institution, and if there are good monitoring mechanisms in place, then there is a good chance that quality will keep a high profile. This makes it harder to ignore, and increases the chances of its being taken seriously.

The strategic plan can help staff understand the institution's mission. It helps to bridge gaps in communication. There is a need for staff to know where their institution is going and how it will be different in the future. Senior management must trust their staff sufficiently to share their vision for the institution's future. Visions are often not shared because of a fear of a loss of status and disempowerment by managers. When coupled with a fear of delegation by managers this can make quality development nearly impossible. Managers have to be able to let their staff take decisions and be willing to see them make honest mistakes.

A potential problem area in many institutions is the role played in it by middle management. They have a pivotal role because they both maintain the day-to-day operation of the institution and act as one of its most important communications channels. They can often block change if they have a mind to or they can act as the leaders of teams spearheading the impetus for quality improvement. Middle managers may not define their role as one of innovation unless senior managements communicate to them their vision of a new future. Senior managers must be consistent in their behaviour when advocating and communicating the message of quality improvement. They cannot say one thing and do another and then expect to engender enthusiasm among their staff or loyalty and commitment in their middle managers. They have to persuade others that new working methods will pay dividends.

Barriers to quality are not the sole prerogative of managers. Many staff fear the consequences of empowerment, especially if things go wrong. They are often comfortable with sameness. They need to have the benefits demonstrated to them. For this reason TQM must avoid being about nothing but jargon and hype. This can easily lead to a loss of interest and to scepticism and cynicism, and to the belief that nothing makes any difference. Many of the barriers to TQM involve an element of fear and uncertainty. Fear of the unknown, of doing things differently, of trusting others, and of making mistakes, are powerful defence and resistance mechanisms. Staff cannot give of their best unless they feel that they are trusted and their views listened to. Deming argues that it is essential when undertaking the quality revolution to 'drive out fear' (see his 14 points in the next chapter).

Chapter 4

Models of Quality – Deming, Juran and Crosby

Adopt the new philosophy.
(The second of W Edwards Deming's 14 points)

Three of the most important writers on quality are W. Edwards Deming, Joseph Juran and Philip B. Crosby. All three have concentrated on quality in manufacturing industry, although all claim that their ideas are equally applicable to service industries. None of them has given much consideration to quality issues in education. Nevertheless, their contribution to the quality movement has been so great that it is difficult to explore quality without recourse to their thinking.

When discussing the ideas of Deming, Juran and Crosby it is necessary to realize that their approaches have their limitations and drawbacks, especially as they were developed in an industrial context. Even so, they are illuminating and can provide direction. There is much that can be learnt from them and be readily adapted to education. It is, of course, perfectly acceptable to mix-'n'-match the ideas of the 'gurus'. As we shall see there is much overlap in their thinking and in the main their general conclusions complement each other.

Deming's philosophy of quality

W Edwards Deming's most important book, *Out of the Crisis*, was published in 1982. Its aim was nothing less than to 'transform the style of American management'. As he goes on to say in the preface to the book it is 'not a job of reconstruction or revision ... It requires a whole new structure, from foundation upwards' (Deming, 1982, p ix). Deming is concerned about the failure of management to plan for the future and to foresee problems before they arise. He believes that the fire-fighting approach associated with short-term thinking brings about waste and raises costs and hence the price which customers pay. The result is a loss of markets and with it a forfeiture of employment.

Deming sees the problem of quality lying primarily with management. The basic cause of industrial problems is the failure of senior management to plan ahead. His is not a sequence of steps for implementing quality, but rather a series of exhortations to management about what to do and what not to do if the organization wants to prosper. His famous 14 points (see Figure 4.1) are a mixture of the new philosophy of quality and appeals to management to change their approach. This he combines with important psychological insights into the barriers to adopting a quality culture. The emphasis on prevention rather than cure is Deming's unique contribution to an understanding of how to assure the improvement of quality. The 14 points are a digest of his theory of management, while his 'seven deadly diseases' are the barriers which stand in the way of quality improvement.

The seven 'deadly diseases' or barriers to a new style of management are very much rooted in American industrial culture and two – excessive medical costs and the prohibitive and unproductive costs of litigation – have no relevance for us. However, three in particular are of considerable significance in the educational context, for they help analyse the reasons which can prevent the new thinking from emerging. The first disease is a lack of constancy of purpose. Deming believes that this is the most crippling disease which prevents many organizations adopting quality as a management objective. It is linked closely with his second barrier – short-term thinking. The switching of the emphasis to a long-term vision and the development of a culture of improvement are what he advocates in their place. Educationalists who have faced so many changes of direction in recent years will find much that is familiar in Deming's emphasis on the need for a long-term coherent strategy.

The third 'deadly disease' concerns the evaluation of an individual's performance through merit ratings or annual review. Deming is an opponent of performance appraisal schemes, and has argued that they lead to short-term solutions and under-performance. Inevitably, appraisal has to be based on measurable outcomes and often these provide a misleading view of what is important in the process. He does not believe that the quality of an employee's contribution can be reduced to measurable results. He also believes that, rather than improving performance, appraisal often has the opposite effect. Staff will concentrate on what is important for gaining a good performance rating rather than developing pride in their work, which is the necessary ingredient for the development of quality. Performance appraisal has the effect of putting staff in competition with each other rather than welding them into teams.

Deming's wholehearted opposition to performance review throws down the gauntlet to teacher appraisal. Institutions who intend to pursue TQM will need to consider very carefully how to blend it with externally imposed schemes of appraisal. Merely because Deming is an opponent of appraisal does not mean that the two are incompatible, but it does require that special consideration is given to the way appraisal is conducted to ensure that it does not lead to the effects abhorred by Deming. The compromise is to ensure that appraisal is always a positive and a developmental process.

The fourth 'deadly disease' is job-hopping. Deming contrasts excessive turnover of executive talent in the West with the stability of employment in Japanese companies. Certainly schools which experience high rates of teacher turnover fully appreciate the impossibility of maintaining any long-term consistency of purpose.

The last of his barriers to quality is management by the use of visible figures. Deming says that this is something that is peculiar to US industry, but schools who are coming to terms with examination-results league tables may feel that there is a similar danger for British education. Deming is concerned that organizations which try to measure success through performance indicators may forget that the real measure of success is happy, satisfied customers.

Figure 4.1 *Deming's 14 points explained*

1. **Create constancy of purpose for improvement of the product and service, with the aim to become competitive and to stay in business, and to provide jobs.** Deming believes that too many organizations have only short-term goals and are not looking 20 or 30 years ahead. They need to have long-term plans based on a vision for the future and new innovations. They should seek to meet the constantly changing needs of their customers.

2. **Adopt the new philosophy.** Organizations can no longer compete if they continue to live with the commonly accepted levels of delay, mistakes, defective materials and faulty products. They have to make the shift and adopt new ways of working.

3. **Cease dependence on mass inspection to achieve quality.** Inspection does not improve or guarantee quality. You cannot inspect quality into products. Instead, Deming argues management should provide their staff with training in the statistical tools and techniques necessary for them to monitor and develop their own quality.

4. **End the practice of awarding business on the basis of price.** For Deming price has no meaning without a measure of the quality being purchased. The practice of awarding contracts solely to the lowest bidder can lead to expensive mistakes. This is particularly the case when a large part of the value of the product is supplied from outside contractors. The quality of the final product is dependent on the quality of the inputs. The total quality way is to develop close and long-term relationships with a small number of suppliers, and preferably a single supplier, and to work with them on the quality of components.

5. **Improve constantly and forever the system of production and service, to improve quality and productivity, and thus to constantly decrease costs.** It is the task of management to lead the improvement process and ensure that there is a continual process of improvement in operation.

6. **Institute training on the job.** The greatest waste in an organization is a failure to use the talents of its people properly. Money spent on training the workforce is important, but it is equally important to train against a fixed standard of what is acceptable work. Training is a powerful tool of quality improvement.

7. **Institute leadership.** Deming says that 'the job of management is not supervision, but leadership'. This means a shift away from

traditional management concerns with outcomes – performance indicators, specifications and appraisals – and a move towards a leadership role which encourages improvements to the processes of producing better goods and services.

8. **Drive out fear, so that everyone may work effectively for the company.** Security is the basis on which staff motivation depends. Deming believes that people genuinely want to do a good job providing they work in an environment which encourages them.

9. **Break down the barriers between departments.** People in different departments need to be able to work together as a team. The organization must not be allowed to have units or departments pulling in different directions.

10. **Eliminate slogans, exhortations, and targets, asking for new levels of productivity without providing the workforce with the methods to do the job better.** Exhortations to work harder represent an abrogation of the job of a manager. Slogans and targets for staff have little practical effect. Most of the problems in production are systemic and it is the responsibility of management to sort them out.

11. **Eliminate work standards that prescribe numerical quotas.** Quality cannot be measured by concentrating solely on the output of the processes. Working to numerical quotas often leads to cutting corners and to a diminution of quality.

12. **Remove the barriers that rob people of their right to pride of workmanship.** This requires the abolishing of appraisal systems and merit ratings. Deming has taken a strong position against appraisal systems which he believes put staff in competition with each other and act against teamwork.

13. **Institute a vigorous programme of education and self-improvement.** The more people know the more they can do. The better educated staff are the better able they will be to undertake quality improvements.

14. **Put everyone in the company to work to accomplish the transformation.** The transformation to a quality culture is everybody's job. It is also the single most important task of management.

Quality failure

Deming on the causes of quality failure

If managers are to take seriously the demands of quality they must understand the reasons for quality failure. An important feature in Deming's work has been the analysis of the causes of quality failure. It is necessary to understand the causes of problems if they are to be tackled successfully. He distinguishes between 'common' and 'special' causes of failure. Common causes are those that are attributable to systems failure. These systemic problems are internal to the processes of the institution. They can only be solved or reduced in scale if changes are made to the systems, processes and procedures. The other causes of failure he calls 'special or assignable causes'. These produce non-random variations within the system, and the causes are external to it.

Common causes of quality failure in education

Common causes of poor quality in education can arise from a variety of sources including poor curriculum design, unsuitable and poorly maintained buildings, poor working environment, unsuitable systems and procedures, insufficiently creative timetabling, a lack of necessary resources, and insufficient staff development. If the cause of a fault or failure can be identified as resulting from a systems, policy or resource problem then it is a 'common cause' failure. The management implication is that to remove the cause of the problem systems and procedures need to be improved, reorganized or respecified. This may require a change of policy or perhaps the instigation of a new training programme. The important point to note is that it is only management who can put right such problems. Only they have the authority to make policy or to redesign systems. Other staff may see the necessity of change but implementation will only happen if management takes action. In order to decide the origin and generality of a problem it is necessary to keep data on the extent of failures and to monitor them regularly. Too often in education low attainment is not sufficiently researched and analysed and the causes of failure are not the subject of managerial action.

Special causes of quality failure

Special causes of failure, on the other hand, often arise from procedures and rules not being followed or adhered to, although they may also be attributable to a communications failure or simply to misunderstandings. They may also be the result of an individual member of staff not possessing the necessary skills, knowledge and attitudes required to be a teacher or an educational manager. The special causes of quality problems could include lack of knowledge and skill on the part of particular members of staff, lack of motivation, communications failures, or problems with particular pieces of equipment.

If a problem can be traced to a 'special' cause then it can be put right without the upheaval of a new policy or redesigning the system. Altering systems would be inappropriate and could lead to greater failure. The particular source of failure needs identification and dealing with. Tackling special causes is also the responsibility of management. It is perfectly possible for other members of staff to deal with them, but often they lack the authority to tackle them. Many of the 'special' problems in education arise from a small number of individuals who lack the motivation or skills to be effective teachers. Only management has the authority to find the appropriate solution in these instances.

The role of managers in tackling failure

The implications of this distinction between common and special causes are very important to managers. Does a quality failure result from a non-random special cause, which may be one-off, or does a common cause problem require a change to the institution's policies, systems and procedures? There is no point in having employee motivational programmes to solve problems which no amount of motivation can solve. Too often faults and problems are put down to failures by individuals when, in fact, the difficulties result from deficiencies in policies and systems. Systemic problems can only be dealt with by those who can redesign faulty systems. The vast majority of problems are the result of poor management or inadequate management systems.

Establishing the cause of quality failure and rectifying it is a key task of managers. Too often the wrong people are left to solve problems or inappropriate solutions are taken to correct faults. Far too often individuals are blamed for consequences not of their making, or the wrong people at the wrong level are left to solve problems without the authority to solve the root causes. In such instances they become frustrated when their efforts fail. Deming's simple but important distinction provides an important insight in dealing with quality failures. Deming is very clear that in the vast majority of cases when things go wrong it is not the staff who are to blame, although too often it is teachers who are seen as the scapegoats for failures in the education system. It is often said in the TQM literature that successful quality improvement requires management commitment. That commitment is not just support for the efforts of others. In practical terms it means recognizing that when things go wrong the responsibility for finding a solution always lies with management.

Joseph Juran's project management

Joseph Juran, along with Deming, is the other pioneer of the quality revolution in Japan. Like Deming he was until recently more highly regarded in Japan than in his native USA. In 1981 the Emperor of Japan awarded him the prestigious Order of the Sacred Treasure. He is the author and editor of a number of books including *Juran's Quality Control Handbook*, *Juran on Planning for Quality*, and *Juran on Leadership for Quality*. Juran is most renowned for coining the phrase 'fitness for use or purpose'. The importance of this idea is that a product or service can meet its specification and yet not be fit for its purpose. The specification may be faulty or it may not accord with what the customer wants. Meeting specifications may be a necessary condition of quality in most instances but it is not a sufficient one.

The 85/15 rule

Juran was the first management 'guru' to deal with the broader management issues of quality. He believes, like Deming, that most quality problems can be traced back to management decisions. When considering the role of leadership in quality the 85/15 rule of Joseph Juran is instructive. Juran's rule of thumb is that 85 per cent of an organization's quality problems are the result of poorly designed processes. Putting the systems right can often mean putting the quality right. It follows from this, says Juran, that 85 per cent of problems lie with management, as they have control of 85 per cent of the systems in an organization.

Strategic quality management

To assist managers in planning quality Juran has developed an approach which he calls Strategic Quality Management. SQM is a three-part process based on staff at different levels making their own unique contributions to quality improvement. Senior management has the strategic view of the organization; middle managers take an operational view of quality; while the workforce is responsible for quality control. This is an idea which has a ready application to education and which closely matches the ideas which Consultants at Work have developed for improving quality in further education. John Miller and his associates at Consultants at Work argue that senior managers and governors need to take the strategic quality management role by setting out the college's vision, priorities and policies. Middle managers – heads of department/faculty – are responsible for quality assurance, which involves them in co-ordinating information from course teams, systematically checking on effectiveness, and transmitting the results of monitoring both to course teams and to senior management. Quality control is exercised by teachers operating in course teams who design the characteristic and standards of programmes of study so that they conform to the needs of their learners.

The Juran Institute, which provides consultancy based on Juran's principles, preaches a project-by-project team-solving approach to quality improvement. Quality improvement only has meaning in practical application, and those applications are of the project variety. Juran has said that 'All quality improvement takes place project by project and in no other way' (Juran, 1989, p 78).

Philip Crosby's 14 steps to quality

Philip Crosby's name is associated with two very appealing and powerful ideas in quality. The first is the idea that quality is free, by which he means that there is so much waste and inefficiency in most systems that the savings from quality improvement programmes pay for themselves. The second idea associated with him is the notion that errors, failures, waste, and delay – all the 'unquality things' – can be totally eliminated if the institution has the will. This is his controversial notion of zero defects. Both ideas are very appealing in education. The idea that quality improvement can pay for itself and can lead to an elimination of failure, especially if this could mean pupil and student failure, is one that few institutions can ignore. Crosby, like all the other 'gurus' is at great pains to emphasize that the route to zero-defects is a difficult although achievable one. As he has written 'Quality is free. It's not a gift, but it is free. What costs money are all the unquality things – all the actions that involve not doing jobs right the first time' (Crosby, 1979, p 1).

Crosby's improvement programme is one of the most practical and detailed guides available. Unlike Deming's more philosophical approach, Crosby's model can be followed as a plan of action. Crosby is a popularist writer and his approach is essentially practical. In *Quality Is Free* Crosby outlines his view that a systematic drive for quality will pay for itself. He says that it is non-conformance problems which lead to scrap, rework, refits, tests and inspection. These are the costs of quality. Savings come from doing things right. In education, parallels can be seen with the cost and effort of retake examinations and the generally low success rate associated with them.

Zero defects

Zero defects is Crosby's major, but controversial, contribution to thinking on quality. It is a powerful idea. It is the commitment to success and the elimination of failure. It involves putting systems in place which ensure that things are always done in the right way first time and every time. Crosby argues that aiming for zero defects, in a business context, will increase profits by saving on costs. The impact of quality on the bottom line is what makes Crosby's model so attractive. Crosby does not believe in statistically acceptable levels of quality. For Crosby there is only one standard, and that is perfection. His is a pure prevention model, and he believes that it is possible to deliver error-free work. Other theorists like Deming and Juran do not believe this to be a feasible goal. They argue that it becomes progressively harder to remove errors the closer that one gets to zero defects. Juran, for instance, argues that after a certain point conforming to requirements can actually impose additional costs.

Zero defects is a concept which is harder to apply to services than to manufacturing. In services zero defects is desirable, but it is difficult to guarantee fault-free service with so many opportunities for human error. Nevertheless, zero defects is an important service-industry goal. It is an idea which ought to have an important echo in education. At its simplest and most powerful it would mean that all pupils and students would make a success of their education and fulfil their potential. The task of quality improvement in education would be building the systems and structures to ensure that this happened. Much stands in the way of zero defects, particularly norm-referenced examinations which make the goal of zero defects an impossibility and a widely held view that standards can only be maintained by a high degree of failure.

Crosby's programme

The essential first step in a quality programme, according to Crosby, is *Management Commitment*. This is crucial to success and is a point agreed on by all the quality 'gurus'. The quality initiative must be sanctioned and led by senior management. Crosby suggests that this commitment is communicated in a quality policy statement, which needs to be short, clear and accessible. The second step builds on the commitment with the setting up of a *Quality Improvement Team*. Since every function within the organization is a potential contributor to defects and quality failures it follows that every part of the organization must participate in the improvement effort. The Quality Improvement Team has the task of setting and directing the programme which will be implemented across the organization. This team does not do all the quality work. The task of implementing improvements is the responsibility of teams within individual departments. The plan which the Quality Improvement Team draws up must be accepted and endorsed by senior management.

An important task of the Quality Improvement Team is to decide how to specify quality failure and improvement, and this leads into Step 3, *Quality Measurement*. It is important to be able to measure the current and potential nonconformance in such a manner that it permits objective evaluation and corrective action. The types of measurement vary between manufacturing and service organizations, and typically, they include data from inspection and test reports, statistical data, and feedback data from customers. A major contributor to quality measurement is provided in Step 4 by quantifying *The Cost of Quality*. The cost of quality consists of such things as the cost of things going wrong, rework, scrap, having to do things again, inspection, and testing. It is important to be able to identify the costs of quality and to put a value on them. How the costs of quality could be approached in education is discussed in Chapter 11.

Step 5 in Crosby's steps to quality is the building of *Quality Awareness*. It is necessary to raise the awareness of everyone within the organization of the costs of quality and the need to implement a quality improvement programme. This requires regular meetings between management and employees to discuss specific problems and means of overcoming them. Information about the quality programme needs to be communicated. Crosby does not go for the big bang approach to introducing quality. He argues that quality awareness should be low-key and linked to a constant stream of events. Once awareness has been raised it is possible to move on to Step 6, *Corrective Action*. Supervisors need to work with staff to eliminate poor quality. A systematic methodology is required to deal with problems. Crosby suggests setting up a series of task teams with a carefully constructed agenda for action. Reports of the task teams should be fed up the chain of command in a regular series of meetings. To decide which problem to tackle first he suggests applying the Pareto rule. This suggests that 20 per cent of the processes cause 80 per cent of the problems. The biggest problems need to be tackled first followed by the next most important and so on. One way of highlighting the improvement process is through Step 7, *Zero Defects Planning*. He argues that a zero defects programme should be introduced and led by the Quality Improvement Team which is also responsible for its implementation. Crosby argues that all staff should sign a formal contract or pledge to work towards zero defects.

Step 8 emphasizes the need for *Supervisor Training*. It is important that all managers understand their role in the improvement process and this is carried out through a formal training programme. This is particularly important for staff carrying out crucial middle-management roles. Step 9 is the holding of a *Zero Defects Day*. This is a day-long event which establishes the idea of zero defects and informs employees that there has been a change. This is essentially a jamboree to highlight and celebrate the work being carried out on quality and to emphasize the management's commitment to it. It has a more serious side, which is staff development.

Step 10 is *Goal Setting*. Once the pledges to work towards zero defects have been made and the idea has been launched on Zero Defects Day it is important that individual action plans are completed. The goals which teams set themselves must be specific and measurable. Goal-setting leads naturally into Step 11, *Error-Cause Removal*. There needs to be a means by which individual employees can communicate to management the situations which make the pledges difficult to implement. This is best achieved by designing a standard form which goes to the appropriate line manager. All such forms must receive a reply within a particular time period.

It is important to appreciate those who participate in the improvement exercises, Crosby says in his twelfth step, *Recognition*. People, he argues, do not work for money, and once their salary is established something more important takes over. What staff need is a recognition of their achievement and contribution. Crosby argues that the recognition needs to be linked to previously set goals. The awards can be prizes or certificates. Recognition, not money, is what is important.

Crosby's step 13 is the establishment of *Quality Councils*. This is an institutional structure also favoured by Juran. It is important to bring the quality professionals together to decide how problems can best be tackled. Inspectors and quality controllers need a consistent and professional approach to their work. Part of the role of the Quality Council is to monitor the effectiveness of the programme and to ensure that the improvement process continues – which is emphasized in Step 14, *Do It Over Again*. The quality programme never ends. Once goals are reached the programme needs to start over again.

Chapter 5
BS5750 and ISO9000

The customer needs the assurance and confidence that the supplier has the ability to provide the product or service consistently to the defined quality.
(Quality Systems, BS5750, Part 4, 1990, p 4)

BS5750 and ISO9000

Considerable interest has recently been shown in education circles in British Standard 5750 and its international equivalent ISO9000. It is an interest which is taking place on both sides of the Atlantic. As some 17,000 British companies are BS5750 registered it is probably not surprising that educationalists are considering whether this quality standard has a place in their institutions. The growth of the Education Business Partnership movement has stimulated a great deal of interest in business methodologies including BS5750. In this chapter two questions will be considered. First, is BS5750 applicable to education? Second, is it a standard which assists with the creation of a TQM culture?

It is only comparatively recently that education has shown any interest in BS5750, although it has to be said, too, that neither the British Standards Institution nor the International Standards Organization showed much interest in education before 1989. The vast majority of registered BS5750 firms are in manufacturing, but increasingly service industries and professional practices, such as solicitors, architects and management consultants, are gaining registration. There is insufficient educational practice to provide a definitive answer to the appropriateness of BS5750/ISO9000 to education. Only a small number of FE colleges and private training organizations have gained registered firm status, although the interest has now spread to both higher education and schools.

Why should education consider BS5750?

BS5750 and ISO9000 are potentially powerful marketing tools for an organization which can display the registration logo (sometimes inaccurately referred to as a kitemark, which is actually a product quality symbol). It could also place an FE or HE institution in a monopoly provider position if BS5750/ISO9000 is insisted upon by a local Training and Enterprise Council or Scottish Local Enterprise Company for training contracts. BS5750 is identical with the European standard EN29000, the international quality standard ISO9000, and the US quality standard Q90. This comparability is an additional bonus for institutions pursuing international connections or contracts. It is less certain what advantages schools might gain from registration. The main one would be the discipline of having specified and documented their quality system and having a third party accreditation for it.

What are BS5750 and ISO9000?

BS5750 was first published in 1979 under the title *Quality Systems*. It has its origins in the Ministry of Defence and NATO systems, known as AQAP (Allied Quality Assurance Procedures), required by these bodies in their roles as procurement agencies. It is in four parts. Part 1 is applicable to organizations for whom the design and development of products or processes is an important part of their business. An example of an organization seeking accreditation for Part 1 is the Business and Technology Education Council, as their business involves the design of qualifications. Part 2 applies to the majority of organizations and is seen by BSI to be applicable to most educational institutions. It is available for those organizations involved in production or installation. For those organizations involved in inspecting or testing products Part 3 is the requisite part. Part 4 of the standard is a guide to the other three parts. BS5750 Part 1 is identical to ISO9001, Part 2 to ISO9002, etc.

The BS5750/ISO9000 series are known as third-party certification schemes. First-party assessment is where an organization assesses its own quality against its own set of standards. The problem with this, it is claimed, is that the customer may not necessarily have confidence in the assurance process as there is no objective external assessment. To overcome this it is common for large purchasers to send their own assessors to verify the systems of their suppliers. This is known as second-party assessment and is the well-known method used by Marks and Spencer, and the Ministry of Defence, among others. The problems with second-party assessment are obvious, especially if the purchaser is a small organization. Third-Party certification involves an organization working to externally generated national standards which are audited and assessed by qualified assessors.

An institution can, of course, devise its own quality assurance system. BS5750/ISO9000 is not inherently better than anything that can be internally devised. The advantage of BS5750/ISO9000 is that they have external validation and recognition. Many large multi-nationals impose more rigorous standards on their suppliers. Ford, for example, have their standard Q-101, and Nissan their 'the Nissan Way'. BS5750 and ISO9000 are not, therefore, the last words on quality. They do not, for example, have requirements which relate to health and safety, equal opportunities, teamwork, human resource management, and the effect of the organization's activities on the environment and its local community.

The philosophy behind BS5750 and ISO9000

The philosophy behind both BS5750 and ISO9000 is that quality should be built into the systems and procedures of the organization. Post-production inspection is by itself not sufficient to ensure quality. The establishment of a quality assurance system will put the emphasis on prevention rather than cure. Quality is built in at each stage from design, through to purchasing, production, marketing and distribution through a formal and rigorous management system to ensure conformance of the product or service to its specification. The aim is to produce a consistent output which is 'fit for purpose'.

All the activities necessary to produce the good or service require documented procedures if the quality system is to conform to BS5750/ISO9000. An educational establishment would, for example, need to document every activity concerned with the delivery of its programmes, including selection, interviewing, induction, discipline, assessment, records of achievement, advice and guidance, etc. BS5750 and ISO9000 place a considerable discipline on those intending to use them. Putting a system in place is not easy or straightforward. It involves a considerable investment of resources and staff time. Everybody in the institution needs to understand its implications and to work to the systems and follow the procedures which have been put in place. Many teachers might consider the emphasis on following detailed written instructions stifling to initiative and excessively bureaucratic.

Does BS5750 guarantee quality?

BS5750/ISO9000 only sets the standard for the quality system. It does not set the standards which the institution or its learners should be achieving. The staff of the institution together with its customers and those to whom it is accountable are the arbitrators of standards of teaching and learning. What BS5750/ISO9000 does is to assure that there are systems in place to deliver those standards once they have been decided.

BS5750/ISO9000 cannot guarantee consistency of standards between institutions. This is an important consideration because so much attention is given in British education to the question of the consistency of standards. BS5750 and ISO9000 were developed in the commercial environment where the market place is seen as determining standards and value for money.

Auditing quality systems

The auditing of the quality system is carried out by both internal auditors and external lead assessors, and for the external audit there is a fee. A number of accreditation bodies can undertake the audit. Accreditation bodies are overseen by National Accreditation Council for Certification Bodies and are registered with the Department of Trade and Industry as being fit to undertake audits. The bodies which have shown an interest in education and training are BSI Quality Assurance, Lloyds Register Quality Assurance, and Yardsley Quality Assurance. Organizations whose quality systems meet the BS5750/ISO9000 specification achieve registered firm status with the DTI, and can use the accreditation bodies' quality systems logo for marketing and publicity purposes. The standard is awarded for a fixed period, typically three years, at the end of which a new external audit is required. During the period between external audits the organization must carry out its own internal audits. If an organization cannot maintain its systems and procedures to the level of the Standard then registration can be withdrawn. This is more serious than it sounds, as the Department of Trade and Industry maintains a list of organizations who have lost their registration. If an institution decides to pursue the Standard it has to make a long-term commitment to maintaining it.

Applying BS5750 and ISO9000 to education

BS5750/ISO900 is new to education. BSI issued guidance on applying the Standard to education and training only in 1992. ISO does not yet have guidelines for education and training although it is in the process of developing them. Because of its manufacturing origins the language used in the Standard is quite unfamiliar to most people in education. It needs considerable translation for the educational context.

One of the underlying concepts of the Standard is that a quality system must be able to assure the production of products of consistent quality. This presents a methodological problem in education where the 'products', however defined, cannot be produced to a measurably consistent standard regardless of the efficacy of the quality system. Originally BSI insisted that the student (or the value added to the student) was the 'product' of the process. However, under pressure from those who argued that the student is not the product but the primary customer, it has subsequently been agreed that the programme of courses and/or the learning process also qualify as 'products'. However, whatever 'product' definition is adopted it is still not possible to consistently produce an educational 'product'. The problem is that in education, in common with other service industries, the interaction between the customer and the supplier alters the quality of service being provided. All teachers know that no two classes are identical because of the individuals who make them up, and the nature of the interactions in the classroom, laboratory or workshop. It is simply not possible to deliver a consistent level of value-added to all pupils and students and a consistently uniform learning experience. The motivations and attitudes of learners are an important aspect of the quality of the education they receive.

An institution's quality system needs to confront this problem, and it is a difficult one to deal with. Quality policies and implementation strategies need to recognize the effect which student/staff interactions have on the consistency of service delivery. For this reason many people have argued that schools, colleges, and universities might do better to leave BS5750/ISO9000 alone and wait for the publication of a service industry standard, which may offer a more sympathetic approach to the problem of service quality consistency. Time-scales are clearly important, but the issue of the 'product' or the outcomes from the learning process will clearly need to be addressed in an institution's quality policy statement. A practical way of addressing this problem is not to focus directly on the learning process but on the level of entitlement which the learner might expect from the institution, and to build systems which provide a consistent level of entitlement. If the entitlements are closely defined they will have an important direct influence on the learning process without the need to look for consistency in the interactions which take place during that process.

Typically, in industry it takes 18 months to undertake the necessary work for BS5750/ISO9000 registration. The initial small number of FE colleges who have gained registration have also taken about 18 months to achieve it. The workload and cost of achieving the standard should not be underestimated.

Figure 5.1 *BS5750/ISO9000 – A translation for education*

BS5750/ISO9000 Part Requirements Main section heading	Translation for Education
1. Management Responsibility	Management's Commitment to Quality
2. Quality System	Quality System
3. Contract Review	Contracts with Internal & External Customers (Student/pupil entitlements, and the entitlements of the external customers eg Parents)
4. Document Control	Document Control
5. Purchasing	Selection & Admissions Policy
6. Purchaser Supplied Product	Pupil/Student Support Services, including Welfare, Counselling and Pastoral & Tutorial Arrangements
7. Product Identification & Traceability	Records of Pupil/Student Progress
8. Process Control	Curriculum Development, Design & Delivery – Teaching & Learning Strategies
9. Inspection and Testing	Assessment & Testing
10. Inspection, Measuring & Test Equipment	Consistency of Assessment Methods
11. Inspection & Test Status	Assessment Records and Procedures including Records of Achievement
12. Control of the Nonconforming Product	Diagnostic Procedures & Methods of Identifying Underachievement & Failure
13. Corrective Action	Corrective Action for Pupil/Student Underachievement and Failure. The System for Dealing with Complaints and Appeals
14. Handling, Storage, Packaging & Delivery	Physical Facilities & Environment, Other Entitlements Offered eg Sports Facilities, Clubs & Societies, Students' Unions, Drop-In Learning Facilities, etc
15. Quality Records	Quality Records
16. Internal Quality Audits	Validation Procedures & Internal Quality Audits
17. Training	Staff Training and Development, including Procedures for Assessing Training Needs & Evaluating the Effectiveness of Training
18. Statistical Techniques	Methods of Review, Monitoring & Evaluation

The relationship between BS5750/ISO9000 and TQM

The relationship between TQM and BS5750/ISO9000 is a topic of considerable debate. The actual relationship between TQM and BS5750/ISO9000 will be peculiar to each institution. TQM does not force off-the-peg solutions. Each educational institution has its own unique culture, its own needs and has to operate in a particular external environment. However, it needs to be stated that whereas TQM and BS5750/ISO9000 can easily co-exist and each extend the other, one does not require the other. BS5750/ISO9000 is not a TQM standard. TQM is a larger enterprise than establishing a quality system and does not necessarily require the application of an external standard.

There are a number of possible ways of looking at the links between TQM and BS5750/ISO9000. In *Total Quality Management* Peter Hingley and I identified four models of the relationship between BS5750/ISO9000 and TQM (see Sallis and Hingley, 1992, pp 50–1). These are:

The *'first-step model'*, which sees BS5750/ISO9000 as the starting point for TQM. BS5750/ISO9000 can be an attainable first step on the road to total quality. BS5750/ISO9000 tackles the procedural infrastructure which precedes the more difficult changes of culture and attitudes. Obtaining BS5750 or ISO9000 provides the institution with 'kitemarked confidence' to go forward to tackle the larger issues associated with TQM. There are plenty of industrial examples of companies using BS5750/ISO9000 in this way.

The *second model* is closely aligned to the first. It positions BS5750/ISO9000 at the heart of total quality. In this model BS5750/ISO9000 holds TQM in place and provides it with a solid foundation for continuous improvement.

In the *third model* BS5750/ISO9000 has a minor role in the larger TQM enterprise. BS5750/ISO9000 is seen as only one element in a more important venture. Its role is little more than a useful means of assuring the operational consistency of the institution's procedures. In this model quality is delivered by the active participation of the workforce in improvement teams and not by paper-based procedures.

The *fourth model* takes a different view of the relationship between TQM and external quality standards. In this model BS5750/ISO9000 is considered as either irrelevant or even antithetical to the pursuit of quality. BS5750/ISO9000 is viewed as a bureaucratic intrusion into the world of education. BS5750/ISO9000 has aroused some strong and hostile feelings. It is considered by some observers as at best a costly distraction, and at worst an anti-educational concentration on bureaucracy at the expense of desirable goals concerned with learning. The industrial language of the Standard does not help its case. At first reading the language appears to have little relevance to education and needs considerable translation to make it relevant. There is a concern that a rigidly applied BS5750/ISO9000 system could be counterproductive in occupations with professional and well-educated workforces, like teaching. The concern is whether the extra workload and the need to work strictly to systems and procedures, albeit internally generated, could damage staff morale and creativity.

Individual institutions will need to clarify the relationship between TQM and BS5750/ISO9000 for themselves. The acid test is the kind of system which the institution's customers want or demand from it. Once an institution is clear about why it is pursuing quality it needs to consider whether a formal quality system will assist it in achieving its goals. The choice of a system is not entirely a matter of fancy. There is a difference between wanting to introduce a quality assurance system and being able to do so. Introducing BS5750 or ISO9000, as previously discussed, is an expensive and time consuming affair, and may be beyond the pocket of many smaller institutions, particularly schools. The costs are up-front and substantial, while any benefits are likely to be mainly long-term.

Chapter 6
Other Quality 'Kitemarks'

Quality management is needed because nothing is simple any more, if indeed it ever was.
(Crosby, 1979, p 19)

As we have seen, quality marks and quality standards may have a role to play in TQM. They can give important messages to customers, actual and potential, that the institution takes quality seriously, and that its policies and practices conform to national and international standards of quality. This can provide considerable external confidence as well as building internal pride. A great deal of attention has been given to BS5750 and ISO9000 recently, but there are alternative quality marks and standards in existence, which could be pursued.

BS4891 Guide to Total Quality Management

The British Standards Institution is developing advice and direction on TQM in BS7850 British Standard Guide to Total Quality Management. BS7850 will not be a Standard, and it is not envisaged as having a system of third-party assessment as BS5750 has. BS7850 is not designed to be prescriptive. It is a guide to the type of approach and methodology which an organization pursuing TQM might adopt.

The definition of TQM is one which emphasizes the participation and co-operation of all employees in the production of a good or service. The purpose is to ensure that customers are satisfied with the goods and services and that society as a whole benefits.

The Foreword to the draft Standard has an interesting section on the initial investment needed for TQM. It lists the following investments as being central for the implementation of TQM – investment in time and people; time to train people; time to implement new concepts; time for people to recognize the benefits; and time for people to move forward into new and different company cultures.

BS7850 has two parts. Part 1 covers management processes, and Part 2 quality improvement. Part 1 contains advice on mission statements, management commitment, customer satisfaction, quality losses, participation by all, process measurement, problem identification, personal development, creating appropriate organizational structures, measurement of performance, training, and tools and techniques. Part 2 amplifies the themes of Part 1 and gives more detail on the methodology and measurement of quality improvement. It also contains a useful guide to the available tools that can be applied to assist the process of quality improvement. Educational institutions will find it a useful and ready guide when implementing TQM.

Investors in People

Investors in People (IIP) was launched in October 1991. It is different from BS5750. It is a standard for human resource development and training and as such it sits easily alongside TQM. Investors in People is overseen by the Department of Employment and its standards have been developed by the National Training Task Force. It is administered and assessed locally by Training and Enterprise Councils and Local Enterprise Companies in Scotland, except for multi-site companies who are directly assessed by the Department of Employment. Its one drawback is that it is a UK standard without international parallels, and its lack of international recognition may deter some organizations from pursuing it.

Investors in People is based on the experience of successful organizations in the UK who have recognized that a skilled and motivated workforce is crucial to their success. IIP provides a methodology for developing staff in ways which assist in the achievement of organization goals. The essential elements which have to be satisfied for an organization to become an Investor in People are:

- a public commitment from the top to develop all staff to achieve the organization's objectives;
- a written institutional plan which identifies organizational goals and targets. The plan identifies training policy and the resources available for it. The plan has to be openly available and understood by all staff;
- regular reviews of the training and development of all staff;
- action to train and develop individuals throughout their careers;
- evaluation of the investment in training and development and an evaluation of the effectiveness of the staff development process. This is likely to be the most difficult part of the standard to demonstrate. The evidence for the effectiveness of training and development is notoriously difficult to quantify. It is unlikely that subjective judgements will satisfy the external assessors. Measures of success will have to be developed which link the delivery of training to the achievement of institutional goals.

Becoming an Investor in People

The process of implementing IIP is in four stages. The first stage is formal commitment by the institution to the standard. To undertake commitment two important tools are available in the 'toolkit' provided by local TECs and LECs. These tools are the Manager Survey, which is designed for senior managers, and the Employee Survey. The Manager Survey contains a series of statements with a scoring system which enables senior managers to assess their institutions against the national standard. The other tool is the very important Employee Survey. This is a questionnaire for staff which asks their opinion of staff development policies and practices, and surveys their perceptions of the commitment of management to investing in their staff. The employee questionnaire can be modified to suit particular circumstances and most institutions will probably wish to do so to fit it to the educational context. An institution may wish to add extra questions because the opportunity to survey staff formally is a chance which can provide a wealth of important information.

Once the Manager and Employee Surveys have been carried out an action plan has to be drawn up, designed to bridge the gap between the IIP standard and the actual practices and perceptions within the institution. It is at this stage that most organizations decide to commit themselves formally to their local TEC or LEC. The commitment takes the form of a letter from the Headteacher or Principal to the Chief Executive of the TEC or LEC.

The second stage follows from the action plan and is the process of planning the strategies necessary to improve the institution's performance. This will need to be included in the institution's strategic plan and be made available to all staff. This stage is followed by the actions necessary to improve policies, procedures and practice. The final stage is that of evaluation. The 'toolkit' provides a range of useful evaluation tools and provides the criteria against which the institution will be assessed. It should be noted that the existence of a formal appraisal scheme is an important, although not essential, element in providing evidence that the institution is matching its staff development needs to institutional objectives. IIP can be a potentially useful tool for ensuring that appraisal systems become genuinely developmental tools.

As with other quality standards evidence is required by the external auditors who undertake the audit. It is a more flexible and less paper-based audit than that undertaken for BS5750 and ISO9000. The auditors will require documentary evidence of the institution's staff development and personnel policies and practices, but an equally important part of the audit is discussion with members of staff. The institution will need to demonstrate the spirit of IIP not just the existence of a formal system to guarantee it.

Investors in People and education

Investors in People was developed for business but it is readily adaptable to education. After all education is about investing in people. A number of schools, colleges, and institutions of higher education have seen the possibilities in it for their quality development initiatives. The process is one that should appeal to many educational institutions who already have well developed processes for staff development review. The major difficulty is that schools and colleges do not currently have the freedom to spend staff development resources in ways which are entirely consistent with their own strategic goals.

Like BS5750/ISO9000 Investors in People does not guarantee quality. However, it is an important indication that the institution is developing a systematic management process to improve the effectiveness of its most valuable resource – its staff. IIP is concerned with developing all employees and this will mean that institutions will have to give equal attention to the staff development of support staff as well as of academic staff. IIP is not a complete TQM standard, but can be a useful marker along the road to total quality. TQM strategies require vision, commitment and the participation of all employees, good communications and a process of evaluating progress. These are all essential features of Investors in People.

The Deming Prize

The Deming Prize is not available in the UK as it is the Japanese national prize for quality. It is described here to provide an indication of the rigorous quality criteria which are applied annually to find the foremost quality company in Japan. As the Japanese are the world leaders in quality many important lessons can be learnt from the Deming Prize. The Japanese national quality prize was launched in 1951. The Prize fund was established from the royalties of Dr Deming's inaugural lectures in Japan.

Winning the Deming Prize for mastering Total Quality Control has been an obsession for many of the big names in Japanese business. There are several Prize categories. Prizes are awarded to a large corporation, a division, a factory and to medium and small companies. There is also a Deming Prize for individuals who have made an outstanding contribution to statistical theory. In addition there is the Japanese Quality Control Medal, established in 1969, which companies can compete for for five years after winning the Deming Prize. To qualify for a Prize the top management of a company must make the application. Outside experts then carry out an exhaustive quality audit to determine the winner. Many of the household names of Japanese industry have won it, including Toshiba, Toyota, and Komatsu.

The Prize criteria are exceptionally demanding and they have been criticized in a number of quarters as being excessively rigid in their approach to total quality. Nevertheless, the Prize has made a major impact, and it was an important reason why the USA established its own Malcolm Baldridge Award in 1987. The checklist for the Deming Prize covers the following elements – a company's policy and objectives; its organizational structure, including co-operation between divisions and utilization of quality circles; education, including education in quality control, the education of sub-contractors, and education in statistical process control; the use of information, including statistical information; analysis of statistics and results; standardization; control systems, including the contributions of quality circles; quality assurance, including new product development, safety procedures, measurement and inspection; quality audits; the effects of quality improvement, including the environmental impact, delivery dates, serviceability, profit, safety; and the future plans of the company, including its long-range plans.

The Malcolm Baldridge Award

The Malcolm Baldridge Award is the American equivalent of the prestigious Japanese Deming Prize. The Award was established by the US Congress in 1987. Baldridge is not a standard but, like the Deming Prize, an annual competition. The Award is designed to recognize US companies that excel in quality achievement and quality management. The Award is designed to promote the following:

- an awareness of quality;
- understanding of the requirements of quality;
- sharing of information on successful strategies and the benefits derived during implementation.

The Baldridge criteria fit extremely well with the Deming philosophy of quality. Unlike BS5750/ISO9000 there is a strong emphasis on the non-procedural aspects of quality such as leadership, human resource management, including employee well-being and morale, and customer satisfaction. The analysis of the results of the quality improvement process are an important element. Applications are examined against a list of criteria which is regularly updated. The 1991 Examination had four main parts:

The Driver
- Leadership
  Senior Executive Leadership
  Quality Values
  Management for Quality
  Public Responsibility

The System
- Information and Analysis
  Scope and Management of Quality Data and Information
  Competitive Comparisons and Benchmarks
  Analysis of Quality Data and Information
- Strategic Quality Planning
  Strategic Quality Planning Process
  Quality Goals and Plans
- Human Resource Utilization
  Human Resource Management
  Employee Involvement
  Quality Education and Training
  Employee Recognition and Performance Measurement
  Employee Well-Being and Morale
- Quality Assurance of Products and Services
  Design and Introduction of Quality Products and Services
  Process Quality Control
  Continuous Improvement of Processes
  Quality Assessment
  Documentation
  Business Process and Support Service Quality
  Supplier Quality

Measurement
- Quality Results
  Product and Service Quality Results
  Business Process, Operational, and Support Service
  Supplier Quality Results

Goals
- Customer Satisfaction
  Determining Customer Requirements and Expectations
  Customer Relationship Management
  Customer Service Standards
  Commitment to Customers

Complaint Resolution for Quality Improvement
Determining Customer Satisfaction
Customer Satisfaction Results
Customer Satisfaction Comparison

There is some interest in the Baldridge Award in Britain as an internal auditing standard. The criteria cover most of the areas which an inspiring total quality organization needs to address. Many people in education feel that the Baldridge Award, or something like it, may provide the way forward long-term for quality standards in education. It is wide-ranging and has a strong emphasis on vision, leadership and on the improvement process. This can be seen to link more closely to educational process than does BS5750/ISO9000, with the latter's emphasis on systems and procedures. Unfortunately, the Baldridge Award is currently only available for US profit-making organizations. Educational institutions in the USA are not eligible for the Awards. It could, however, prove a useful process for any educational institution to use the Baldridge criteria as the standard against which to measure itself. This could be carried out as part of an internal auditing process.

The European Quality Award

The European Quality Award was launched during the 1991 European Quality Management Forum's meeting in Paris. The Forum is a new organization formed in 1988 by 14 leading Western European companies. It is now made up of some 170 companies who aim to stimulate and assist European companies in their development of total quality. The European Commission is playing a role in its development. The aim of the Forum and of the Award is specifically geared to encourage the development of TQM. The Award aims to recognize organizations who are paying exceptional attention to total quality, and to encourage others to follow their example. The European Quality Award is not a standard but a competition Award like the Japanese Deming Prize and the US Malcolm Baldridge Award. It is a single annual award presented to the most successful exponent of TQM in Western Europe. The first Award was presented in 1992. In addition there are a number of European Quality Prizes for companies who have demonstrated excellence in their management of quality. The criteria for the Award have a distinctive European flavour and are designed to provide a model of excellence for companies regardless of size and type of business. An organization which seeks the Award will be assessed on its results and improved performance achieved under the following headings:

- customer satisfaction;
- employee satisfaction;
- business performance;
- the organization's impact on society.

There are eight specific criteria and their relative values within the overall award are:

- Customer satisfaction – the perceptions of external customers, direct and indirect, of the company and of its products and services (20%)
- People – the management of the company's people and the people's feeling about the company (18%)
- Business results – the company's achievement in relation to its planned business performance (15%)
- Processes – the management of all the value-added activities within the company (14%)
- Leadership – the behaviour of all managers in transforming the company towards Total Quality (10%)
- Resources – the management, utilization and preservation of:
  financial resources
  information resources
  technological resources (9%)
- Policy and strategy – the company's vision, values and direction, and the ways in which it achieves them (8%)
- Impact on society – the perceptions of the community at large, of the company. Views of the company's approach to the quality of life, to the environment and to the need for preservation of global resources are included (6%)

The emphasis of the European Award is: 'Are you trying to do the right things?' It has more emphasis than Baldridge on the impact on society, resource utilization and on business results. As the Award is new it is too early to assess its impact, but the intention is to provide an award in the European Community of comparable status to the Japanese Deming Prize and the US Baldridge Award. The problem with it and other awards is that with only a single annual winner it is likely that its impact will be limited to large corporations. The aim of the Award is clearly to encourage the imitation of excellence exhibited by the Award's winners. The European Quality Award competition can be entered by educational institutions whose education or training provision has a significant European dimension.

The Citizen's Charter

The Citizen's Charter has had wide publicity, and following the 1992 general election it has its own Cabinet Minister. It is a programme designed to improve public services and to give people more choice. It does this by publishing details of what the public can expect from a service and providing them with a clear complaints procedure. The Charter's principles cover all public services including education. In education the first such charter is the Parent's Charter. Linked to the charters is the Charter Mark, which is an award which recognizes excellence in the delivery of public services. Public sector organizations and the privatized utilities can apply for the Charter Mark. Individual schools can apply as they have their own LMS budgets. The Charter Mark is a competition and in the first year of operation, 1992, some 50 were due to be awarded. The Charter Marks are valid for three years and are awarded against a set of criteria. There are six principles in the Charter Standard:

1. Publication of standards of service and performance against those standards.
2. Customer consultation.
3. Clear information about the services.
4. Courteous and efficient customer service.
5. Complaints procedure.
6. Independent validation of performance and a commitment to value for money.

Institutions which apply have to provide evidence of how they perform against the principles of the Charter Mark and demonstrate how continuous improvement is built into their processes. They must demonstrate measurable improvements in performance. They also have to have plans to introduce at least one innovative enhancement to their service at no additional cost to the taxpayer or consumer.

The Parent's Charter contains the recent legislative changes concerned with parental choice and the publication of information, including annual written reports on children's progress, published tables of performance results in tests and examinations, reports of inspections, etc. It currently only applies to schools. The Charter gives parents important rights as consumers. Whether it will serve to improve quality remains to be seen.

Choosing an external quality standard

It is important to remember that the gaining of a quality mark or standard does not guarantee quality. Their importance is that they provide discipline, external assessment, and a clear process through which to pursue quality. They can be a useful milestone for an organization for whom TQM may seem a daunting prospect. They also have tremendous potential publicity value within the institution and with the general public. As the internal marketing of the quality message is vitally important, it can be of great value to celebrate the achievement of gaining a national or international standard.

The competition awards of the Deming Prize, the Malcolm Baldridge Award, and the European Quality Award have more TQM application than BS5750/ISO9000, and a more general application than the training and development standard Investors in People. Some institutions may find it attractive to work towards a Charter Mark under the Citizen's Charter. These competition awards together with BS7850 could be extremely useful as the criteria for internal TQM audits. In the future many educational institutions will be giving serious consideration to them for use internally.

Chapter 7
Some Organizational Considerations

Successful institutions of the future must be as responsive and fluid as the world around them.

Institutional life-cycle theory

Educational institutions are not stationary entities. They exist only so long as they fulfil a useful purpose. They and their environment are in a constant state of change and, to adopt a biological analogy, all institutions have a 'life cycle'. The institutional life or developmental cycle has four main stages. They are formation, growth, maturity, and lastly a stage which can either lead to decline and decay or to renewal and revitalization. The developmental cycle is the same for educational institutions as for any other organization, especially now education operates in a more deregulated environment. Each stage in the life cycle has its own special challenges, and a failure to meet them can lead to disaster. At each stage an institution must change, adapt and develop. TQM, with its powerful ingredients of long-term strategic planning and the involvement of staff in continuous improvement, provides the means of facing up to the challenges at each stage.

Figure 7.1 *Phases of institutional development*

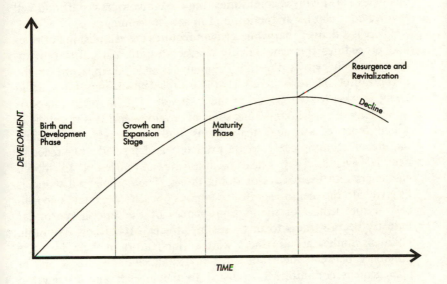

The first stage in the cycle is the birth and formation of the institution. A newly established institution requires a strategy to gain recognition and acceptance. It must establish its niche in the market and find a clientele. The new organization must build a customer base and ensure that it is aware of and is in tune with consumer needs, even if it has created those needs in the first place. The foundation of a new institute is sometimes described as the entrepreneurial phase because the founders are often visionaries, who through personal effort and risk-taking, ensure the institution's future.

If the new organization succeeds it passes into the growth and development stage where it will face new and novel challenges. It has to ensure that it can continue to generate the excitement and optimism which was a strong feature during the formation stage. The main problem, however, in the growth stage is how to cope with the pressures built up by the increased demands for its services. Management systems failure, inabilities to delegate, and the appointment of staff who do not share the ethos of the institution are usual causes of failure. The personal service offered by the young dynamic organization has to be translated into dealing with a much enlarged clientele. This involves communicating the ethos to new staff and will involve considerable induction and in-service training.

There is a danger that while growth requires the establishing of rules and procedures this can quickly degenerate into a needless bureaucracy, which will stifle the original vision and mission of the organization. There is a risk that the organization may move from being market-led to being product driven. The maturity stage is potentially the most dangerous stage of development. It is the stage in which most educational institutions find themselves. Too many mature institutions cease to be proactive and instead only react to external events. They cease to innovate and attempt to mould customers into their ways of doing things. The commercial world is littered with the memories of once famous household names. The roll-call of the demise of the famous names of the British motor-car industry bears witness to this. Austin, Morris, MG, Riley, Triumph, Hillman, Sunbeam and others were all innovators in their day. The difference between them and Nissan, Honda and Toyota is one of management commitment to listen to the market and to develop products which exceed the consumers' expectations. Failure to adapt can swiftly lead to decline and failure. In the new educational market place the same fate can befall educational institutions.

However, the maturity stage can also be one of renewal if the message of total quality is adopted and the institution develops strategies for adaptation and finds ways of keeping close to its customers. It can be a dynamic phase where the experience of the institution can be harnessed for its further development. Maintaining the dynamism and entrepreneurial flair is of major importance when there are rapid changes in the external environment. The institution must periodically reassess its aims and continually evaluate the activities critical to the institution's continual success. In the life-cycle of organizations decline and decay are not inevitable, but the periodic process of revitalization needs to be a conscious exercise.

Traditional and TQM organizations

Institutions with traditional ways of working are finding it increasingly difficult to cope with the pressure of change. Such traditional institutions are usually characterized by departmental barriers, the lack of a common mission, overbearing hierarchies, and an over-reliance on rigid procedures. They will not have developed a customer focus and their pupils and students are more often than not seen as liabilities not assets. Improvements, when they are attempted, usually have as their goal reducing costs. What TQM offers is the opportunity for an institution to take a 180 degree turn. The effective TQM institution has a different outlook, diametrically opposed to the traditional model. It will have integrated quality into its structure and recognizes that quality involves everyone at all levels making their contribution. To achieve this a considerable investment needs to be made in people as they are the keys to quality, and hence to the institution's future.

If a school or college aspires to be a total quality institution it must act like one. It must innovate and drive ahead to achieve the vision contained in its mission statement. It should recognize that quality will always provide an edge in the market. Most important, it must carry the message to its staff and ensure that they are partners in the process. The quality route is by now well trodden but just as hard. The driving force has to come from the top and the process has to be constantly nurtured and reinforced. Leadership is the key, but so is listening and learning. It is often the little things which provide the evidence of quality. Institutions which make the effort to get the details right also have the right approach to the major issues. In a world where so many services look superficially similar it is attention to detail which provides the competitive edge. Above all in the words of Tom Peters, 'Ensure that quality is always defined in terms of the customer perceptions' (Peters, 1987, p 64).

Lean forms and simple structures

There are no correct forms of organization for TQM, although some structures are more suitable than others. Structures need to be appropriate and facilitate the TQM process. The evidence suggests that as TQM develops much of the hierarchy is eliminated, and flatter structures with strong cross-institutional links take their place. The more appropriate organizational forms are simple, lean, and are built

Figure 7.2 *The differences between a quality institution and an ordinary institution*

QUALITY INSTITUTION	ORDINARY INSTITUTION
Customer focused	Focused on internal needs
Focus on preventing problems	Focus on detecting problems
Invests in people	Is not systematic in its approach to staff development
Has a strategy for quality	Lacks a strategic quality vision
Treats complaints as an opportunity to learn	Treats complaints as a nuisance
Has defined the quality characteristics for all areas of the organization	Is vague about quality standards
Has a quality policy and plan	Has no quality plan
Senior management is leading quality	The management role is seen as one of control
The improvement process involves everybody	Only the management team is involved
A Quality Facilitator leads the improvement process	There is no Quality Facilitator
People are seen to create quality – creativity is encouraged	Procedures & rules are all important
Is clear about roles and responsibilities	Is vague about roles and responsibilities
Has clear evaluation strategies	Has no systematic evaluation strategy
Sees quality as a means to improve customer satisfaction	See quality as a means to cut costs
Plans long-term	Plans short-term
Quality is seen as part of the culture	Quality is seen as another and troublesome initiative
Is developing quality in line with its own strategic imperatives	Is examining quality to meet the demands of external agencies
Has a distinctive mission	Has no distinctive mission
Treats colleagues as customers	Has a hierarchical culture

around strong teamwork. Some writers such as Tom Peters sound warnings about elaborate matrix structures with their complexity of linkages which can hinder the process by leading to a 'bloated' organization which becomes concerned with its own maintenance (see Peters, 1987, pp 357–8).

Tall hierarchies with excessive layers of management can make it difficult for those in the classroom to do their job effectively. In its place TQM puts teamwork. The development and strengthening of teamwork, so much a feature of TQM, reduces the need for much of the middle-management controlling and scheduling function. In its place middle managers become the leaders and champions of quality, and take on the role of supporting teams and assisting their development. This new role for middle-managers is important because teamwork can have a downside. Teams which are too autonomous may branch out in uncoordinated and ineffective ways. Teamwork needs to be structured within a simple but effective management system. It is important that teams understand the vision and the policies of the institution. This is one of the reasons why vision and leadership are so heavily emphasized in the TQM literature.

Organizations, from a TQM perspective, are systems designed to serve customers. In order to serve the customers all the parts and systems of the institution must dovetail. The success of any one unit of the organization affects the performance of the whole. The difference between a mature structure operating under TQM and the more usual organizational forms is that traditional organizations are structured around functions while TQM institutions are organized around processes. The idea is that the whole of a process should be under a single and simple chain of command. For example, are all the functions associated with pupil or student support and welfare integrated and under a single source of control? Under TQM, structure follows process, and the following are necessary features of any quality organization:

- Unit optimization – every unit, programme, and department needs to operate efficiently and effectively. Each area needs to have clear, and preferably written, quality standards within which to operate.
- Vertical alignment – every member of staff needs to understand the strategy of the institution, and its direction and mission, although they may not need to know the detailed breakdown of objectives.

- Horizontal alignment – there should be a lack of competition between units/programmes/departments, and an understanding of the aims and requirements of other parts of the organization. Mechanisms need to be in place to deal effectively with any boundary problems.
- A single command for each process – the key processes, whether they are curriculum, pastoral, or administrative – need to be charted and organized so that each process is brought under a single chain of command. The charting process is best carried out from an analysis which starts by asking who the customer for a process is

Figure 7.3 *Institutional alignment*

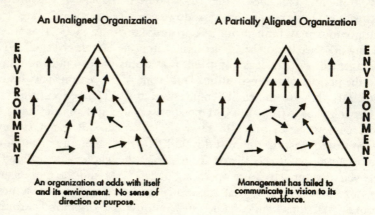

An Unaligned Organization

An organization at odds with itself and its environment. No sense of direction or purpose.

A Partially Aligned Organization

Management has failed to communicate its vision to its workforce.

A Totally Aligned Organization

An organization which is aligned with its environment.

84

and continues by analysing their needs and the standards they should expect.

Structural reorganizations are not a requirement for TQM. Reorganizations may be useful and necessary to the quality improvement process, but equally they can divert attention from quality improvement and lead to institutional fatigue. There are plenty of examples in education where organizational restructuring has impeded quality development. There is usually only so much energy within a system. TQM usually provides as much change as the organization can reasonably cope with. Staff need some familiar signposts while adapting to new working methods. It is sensible to let structural change develop out of the process of improving quality, and so it is probably best to avoid organizational restructuring at the start of the TQM programme.

Chapter 8

Educational Leadership for Quality

Leadership is the essential ingredient in TQM. Leaders must have the vision and be able to translate it into clear policies and specific goals.

The educational leader

Total quality is a passion and a way of life for those organizations who live its message. The question is how to generate the passion and the pride required to generate quality in education. Peters and Austin researched the characteristics of excellence for their book *A Passion for Excellence*. Their research led them to the belief that what makes the difference is leadership. They argue strongly for a particular style of leadership to lead the quality revolution – a style to which they have given the acronym, MBWA or 'management by walking about'. A passion for excellence cannot be communicated from behind the office desk. MBWA emphasizes both the visibility of leaders and their understanding and feeling for the front-line and the processes of the institution. This style of leadership is about communicating the vision and the values of the institution to others, and getting out among the staff and the customers and experiencing the service for themselves.

Peters and Austin gave specific consideration to educational leadership in a chapter entitled 'Excellence in School Leadership'. Their prescription of the qualities required of an excellent educational leader are worth consideration. They see the educational leader as needing the following perspectives:

- **Vision and symbols**. The Headteacher or Principal must communicate the institution's values to the staff, pupils and students and the wider community.
- **'Management by walking about'** is the required leadership style for any institution.
- **'For the Kids'.** This is their educational equivalent to 'close to the customer'. It ensures that the institution has a clear focus on its primary customers.
- **Autonomy, experimentation, and support for failure.** Educational leaders must encourage innovation among their staff and be prepared for the failures that inevitably accompany innovation.
- **Create a sense of 'family'.** The leader needs to create a feeling of community among the institution's pupils, students, parents, teachers, and support staff.
- **'Sense of the whole, rhythm, passion, intensity, and enthusiasm.'** These are the essential personal qualities required of the educational leader.

(See Peters and Austin 1986 pp 393–414.)

The significance of leadership for undertaking the transformation to TQM should not be underestimated. Without leadership at all levels of the institution the improvement process cannot be sustained. Commitment to quality has to be a prime role for any leader. It is for this reason that TQM is said to be a top-down process. It has been estimated that 80 per cent of quality initiatives fail in the first two years. The main reason for failure is lack of senior management backing and commitment. Quality improvement is too important to leave to the quality co-ordinator. To succeed in education TQM requires strong and purposeful leadership.

Typically, managers in non-TQM organizations spend 30 per cent of their time in dealing with systems failure, complaints and with 'fire-fighting'. As TQM saves that time managers have more time to lead, plan ahead, develop new ideas and work closely with customers.

Communicating the vision

Senior management must give the lead and provide vision and inspiration. In TQM organizations all managers have to be leaders and champions of the quality process. They need to communicate the mission and cascade it throughout the institution. Many managers, particularly middle managers, may find total quality difficult to accept and to implement. It involves a change in the management mind-set as well as a change of role. It is a change from the 'I'm in charge' mentality to that of manager as supporter and leader of front-line staff. The function of leadership is to enhance the quality of learning and to support the staff who deliver it. While this sounds obvious it is not always the way management functions are viewed. Traditional notions of status can lie uneasily with the total quality approach. TQM turns the traditional institution on its head and inverts the hierarchy of functions. It empowers the teachers and can provide them with greater scope for initiative. It is for this reason that it is often said of TQM institutions that they requires less management and more leadership.

The role of the leader in developing a quality culture

What is the role of the leader in an institution undertaking a total quality initiative? No list of attributes says it all, but the major functions of leadership are as follows. A leader must:

- have a vision of total quality for his or her institution;
- have a clear commitment to the quality improvement process;
- communicate the quality message;
- ensure that customer needs are at the centre of the institution's policies and practices;
- ensure that there are adequate channels for the voices of customers;
- lead staff development;
- be careful not to blame others when problems arise without looking at the evidence. Most problems are the result of the policies of the institution and not the failings of staff;
- lead innovation within their institutions;
- ensure that organizational structures clearly define responsibilities and provide the maximum delegation compatible with account-ability;

- be committed to the removal of artificial barriers whether they be organizational or cultural;
- build effective teams;
- develop appropriate mechanisms for monitoring and evaluating success.

Empowering teachers

A key aspect of the leadership role in education is to empower teachers to give them the maximum opportunity to improve the learning of their students. Stanley Spanbauer, the President of Fox Valley Technical College, who has taken a lead in introducing TQM into vocational education in the USA, argues that 'in a quality-based approach, school leadership relies on the empowerment of teachers and others involved in the teaching/learning process. Teachers share in decision-making and assume greater responsibilities. They are given more power to act and greater autonomy in almost everything they do.' He goes on to elaborate his belief in the importance of leadership with these words: 'Commitment means much more than giving an annual speech on how important quality is to our school. It requires unending enthusiasm and devotion to quality improvement. It calls for an almost fanatic promotion of and attention to new ways to do things. It requires constant review of each and every action' (Spanbauer, 1992, p 15).

Spanbauer has put forward a plan for leadership to create a new educational environment. He argues that educational leaders should guide and assist others to develop a similar set of characteristics. This encourages shared responsibility and a style which will engender an interactive working environment. He visualizes a leadership style where leaders 'must walk and talk quality and understand that change happens by degree, not by decree' (Spanbauer, 1992, p 16). Leaders have a pivotal role in guiding teachers and administrators to work for and in concert with their client groups. Spanbauer is essentially concerned with leadership for empowerment. His conclusions are:

1. Involve teachers and all staff in problem-solving activities, using basic scientific methods and the principles of statistical quality and process control.
2. Ask them how they think about things and how projects can be handled rather than telling them how they will happen.

3. Share as much management information as possible to help foster their commitment.

4. Ask staff which systems and procedures are preventing them from delivering quality to their customers – students, parents, co-workers.

5. Understand that the desire for meaningful improvement of teachers is not compatible with a top-down approach to management.

6. Rejuvenate professional growth by moving responsibility and control for professional development directly to the teachers and technical workers.

7. Implement systematic and continued communication among everyone involved in the school.

8. Develop skills in conflict resolution, problem-solving, and negotiations while displaying greater tolerance for and appreciation of conflict.

9. Be helpful without having all the answers and without being condescending.

10. Provide education in quality concepts and subjects such as team building, process management, customer service, communication, and leadership.

11. Model, by personally exhibiting desired characteristics and spending time walking around, listening to teachers and other customers.

12. Learn to be more like a coach and less like a boss

13. Provide autonomy and allow risk-taking while being fair and compassionate.

14. Engage in the delicate balancing act of ensuring quality to external customers (students, parents, taxpayers), while at the same time paying attention to the needs of internal customers (teachers, board members, and other co-workers) (Spanbauer, 1992, p 56).

Chapter 9
Teamwork for Quality

Teamwork throughout any organization is an essential component of the implementation of TQM for it builds up trust, improves communication and develops independence.

(John S Oakland, *Total Quality Management*, 1989, p 236)

The importance of teamwork in education

Organizations which become involved in TQM discover the benefits of having effective teams at all levels. In many sectors of education teams have been developed as the basic unit for curriculum delivery and education has a head-start as teamwork is an established fact. This provides educational institutions with a strong platform from which to build TQM cultures.

However, the application of teamwork has often been limited to curriculum and management functions. To build an effective TQM culture teamwork needs to be extended and must penetrate and permeate throughout the institution and be used in a wide range of decision-making and problem-solving situations. It must also exist at all levels. Teamwork needs to extend across all functions and should include both academic and support staff. The divisions between teaching and support staff and between hierarchical grades have often prevented the necessary extension of teamwork and these barriers need to be broken down.

The role of project teams

In TQM establishments teams are not just there to run things. While this is an important function of teams they can also be used to achieve specific projects. *Ad hoc* and short-life project and improvement teams are key elements in the delivery of quality improvements. Teams have the added advantage of involving the maximum number of people in the total quality process. Teams become the engines of quality improvement. It is useful to think of the TQM institution as a series of overlapping teams.

Quality improvement works by a series of teams working on small incremental projects each of which is designed to solve a problem, improve an existing process or design a new one. The brief of each is usually limited because it is easier to achieve success with small and manageable assignments. Small projects which fail do not jeopardize the credibility of the whole process. The idea is that a series of small successful projects can add up to something much larger. The projects need to have a common focus so that there is coherence and direction, with the end result benefiting a particular customer, either internal or external. Initially, the team needs to be tutored in taking methodical approaches and finding permanent and long-lasting solutions. Teams can make use of the TQM tools described in Chapter 10 for solving problems and making decisions.

Teams as the building blocks for quality

As we have seen, the synergy required to make quality improvements comes from people working in harmony. Quality improvement is hard work, and this is best approached with the support of others. Much of the interesting quality work in further education, for example, has centred around developing the role of the course team. The innovative Strategic Quality Management model of Miller, Dower, and Inniss takes the course team as the essential building block for delivering quality in further education. The course team is seen to have a number of important functions which could include:

- being accountable for the quality of learning;
- being accountable for the use of the teachers' time, non-teaching time, and the materials and space which it utilizes;
- being a vehicle for monitoring, evaluating and improving quality;

- acting as a conduit of information to management on the changes necessary to improve provision. The team 'is a powerful means of making and proposing changes'. The team should not be just an instrument for gathering data. It should use the data it gathers to improve the opportunities for its learners.

(see Miller, Dower, and Inniss, 1992, p 15).

Nevertheless, despite the importance of the course team the power of teamwork should not be limited to them. A well-functioning institution should consist of a large number of overlapping teams. Teams should not consist exclusively of academic or support staff. Mixed teams of academic and non-academic support staff have an important role to play. Some teams will have a long life, while others take on short-term tasks.

Teamwork, however, does not just happen. As Philip Crosby has said, 'Being part of a team is not a natural human function; it is learned' (Crosby, 1979, p 126). Training in teamwork and problem-solving skills is often necessary. The members of a team have to learn to work together. Teams are made up of individuals with different personalities, ideas, strengths, weaknesses, levels of enthusiasm, and demands from their jobs. Too often in education, as elsewhere, we just expect teamwork to happen. A group of people work on the same programme and we call them a team. Usually, only the team leadership role is identified, and that is often the only structure the 'team' has. Teams, like people, need nurturing and mentoring if they are to function well and give of their best. Their contribution has to be recognized and supported.

The stages of team formation

Teamwork needs to be based on mutual trust and established relationships. Only when a team has an identity and purpose can it deal effectively with its primary function. Teams do not come ready formed. They have to go through a formation process which is critical to their ability to function properly. Teams need time to grow and mature. B W Tuckman has suggested a four stage growth and maturity cycle for team development. It begins when teams form, and takes them through the stages of growth which he describes as storming, norming, and performing.

Tuckman calls the first stage of group formation 'forming'. At this stage the team is not a team. It is just a collection of individuals. There is a range of emotions associated with this stage, from excitement, optimism, idealism, pride, and anticipation through to fear, suspicion, and anxiety. The main discussions will centre on philosophical issues concerned with concepts and abstractions, or on the organizational barriers to successful working. At this stage the team may easily be distracted and can start dealing with matters outside its remit. Some of its members may be more concerned with stamping their identity on the group than in working on tasks. These patterns of behaviour are often seen as wasteful in time and effort. In fact, they are normal and necessary. They are essential processes which any team must go through. They will be helped if a senior manager can share a vision with them, and can provide them with clear guidelines. The agenda must not be too detailed or it will stifle the inherent creativity of the team. The team's remit should give them direction and a knowledge that management values their efforts.

Some teams never form, but if they do, they proceed to a more difficult second stage known as storming. This can be an uncomfortable period. This is the stage when members realize the scale of the task ahead and may react negatively to its challenges. Others will want to lay down personal agendas. Interpersonal hostilities may arise. It is usual to have arguments about the lack of progress being made and the time which is being wasted. Unless conflicts at this stage are properly handled the team's very existence can easily be curtailed. The team leader must recognize the source of any conflict and diffuse it by assisting members to search for common ground. There is a positive side to the storming stage. It is the period when members begin to understand each other. Humour and patience are important qualities for a team leader at this stage, as are firmness and resolve.

The next stage, norming, is where a team decides and develops its methods of working. The team establishes its own rules or norms, and sorts out the roles which its members should play. If the rules are well defined and understood the team has a good chance of functioning properly. A structured approach to training in teamwork can assist considerably in this stage.

Performing is Tuckman's fourth stage in the process of group formation. The team members have now worked out their differences and established their ways of working and they can start the process of solving problems and improving processes. A fully mature team has been created which can work together and within which the synergy of group working brings rewards. The team will have built up an identity and established 'ownership' of the processes it uses.

There is no typical time-scale for a team to follow this process of development. Even the most experienced team members need a meeting or two to establish themselves as a new team, but if the members are new to teamwork the formation stage will take longer. It is important to remember that even when the performing stage is reached all teams still have their ups and downs.

The effective team

The size of a team can strongly affect its operation. As Paula Tansley points out in her book on *Course Teams – the Way Forward in FE?* the number of staff involved in a course delivery team is not open to choice to the same extent that it might be in industry. This especially applies to teams involved with classroom issues (Tansley, 1989, p 149). It is, therefore, all the more important to ensure that the other parameters of effectiveness are right if the size of the team cannot be controlled. While there is no one 'recipe' for successful teams the following points should be borne in mind:

A team needs the roles of its members to be clearly defined. It is important to know who is leading a team and who is facilitating it. The distinction between the leader and the facilitator is one that is often used in TQM. The leader's role is self-evident. It is the person who provides the mission and the drive to the team. The facilitator or quality consultant has a more novel role. The facilitator assists the team to make the best use of problem-solving and decision-making tools. This role could be carried out by the leader, but it is difficult for a person to combine both roles successfully in the same way that it is difficult both to chair a meeting and to take the minutes. The other important roles within the team include research, note-taking, and external relations.

Teams need clear purposes and goals. A team needs to know where it is going and to have clear goals to achieve. It is important that the team has a say in its mission and sees it as being workable. The task it is set must be achievable or the mountain will be seen as too big to climb. It must also be relevant to the interests of its members. A good way to establish a sense of purpose is to have an initial session which does no more than establish the team's mission.

A team needs the basic resources to operate. The basic resource needs are people, time, space and energy. The last point on energy is important, and is often neglected in discussions on teamwork, especially in the context of improvement teams. It is important to harness the energy of a team and not to over-extend its life.

A team needs to know its accountability and the limits of its authority. Disillusionment results if deliberations are ignored or if the team exceeds its authority or remit. A clear brief of the purpose of the team is necessary before a team begins its work.

A team needs a plan to work to. The plan will contain the terms of reference, the mission, perhaps a flowchart on the steps required to tackle a project, and the resources at the team's disposal.

A team needs a set of rules to work to. These should be simple and agreed by all members. They are an integral part of the norming stage. Their importance is to set high standards of behaviour and to keep the team on course.

A team needs to use the appropriate tools to tackle problems and to arrive at solutions. The techniques described in Chapter 10 such as brainstorming, flowcharting, and force-field analysis are easy to adopt and can be very powerful problem-solving and decision-making tools.

A team needs to develop beneficial team behaviour. Peter R Scholtes has argued that the keys to good teamwork are 'beneficial team behaviours'. These are things which ideally all team members should be able to do, and include the ability to:

- initiate discussions;
- seek information and opinions;
- suggest procedures for reaching goals;
- clarify or elaborate on ideas;
- summarize;
- test for consensus;
- act as gatekeepers: direct conversational traffic, avoid simultaneous conversations, throttle dominant talkers, make room for reserved talkers, keep conversation from digressing;
- compromise and be creative in resolving differences;
- try to ease tensions in the group and work through difficult matters;
- express the group's feelings and ask others to check that impression;

- get the group to agree on standards;
- refer to documentation and data;
- praise and correct others with equal fairness, accept both praise and complaints.

(Scholtes et al, 1988, pp 6–15/6–16)

The importance of good communications is essential within the team in order to nurture these beneficial behaviours. Essential to good communications among members are honesty and integrity. Equally important is a willingness of members to share their feelings openly and not to indulge in hidden agendas. The team leader plays a crucial role here. It is the team leader's role to prevent the team from becoming bogged down, going round in circles, and from being dominated by one or two individuals.

Quality circles

For many people quality is synonymous with quality circles. They are an essential feature of Japanese total quality control methods. The Japanese TQC philosophy is essentially a blending of the statistical process control ideas of Deming, with quality circles. Setsuo Mito in his book *The Honda Book of Management* says of them: 'TQC and QC circle activities have proved effective in raising worker morale and bringing about qualitative improvements in management wherever they are practised anywhere in the world' (Mito, 1990, p 100). The extensive use of quality circles has been much greater in Japan than elsewhere, although they originated in the USA.

Quality circles are considered an essential part of quality processes in Japan, whereas they are not in the West. This may have something to do with their voluntary and after-hours image which does not fit easily into the Western industrial culture. In the West teams and teamwork have been emphasized in place of quality circles. It is interesting that in one of the most influential of US practical guides to TQM *The Team Handbook*, by Peter R Scholtes and contributors, there are no references to quality circles, whereas Kaoru Ishikawa, who was one of the leading Japanese writers on quality, sees them as the basis of the quality improvement process. In his *What Is Total Quality Control?* Ishikawa charts the development of the quality movement in Japan from its origins in the early 1950s through the growth of the quality circle movement. He describes quality circles as small groups based upon mutual trust, which voluntarily perform quality control activities within the workplace, and which use quality control methods and techniques. The aim of quality circles, Ishikawa suggests, is to:

1. Contribute to the improvement and development of the enterprise.
2. Respect humanity and build a worthwhile-to-live happy, and bright workshop.
3. Exercise human capabilities fully, and eventually draw out infinite possibilities (Ishikawa, 1985, p 140).

The only major difference between quality improvement teams and quality circles is voluntarism. This is, however, a principle which Ishikawa believes to be of fundamental importance. He does not believe that quality circles should come under the command of a superior. The voluntarism principle stops some people from becoming too dependent upon others. Strictly, formally designated groups such as course teams cannot be quality circles. Whether there is a real difference between quality circles and teams, or whether it is merely a matter of semantics can be debated. What unites the two is of more importance. Both are based on the idea that there is a synergy to be gained by working together in a structured and self-directed way to improve the service being provided.

Tim Atkinson, writing about experiments with quality circles in further education colleges, also comes to much the same conclusions. He argues that where quality circles have been experimented with they have proved a beneficial means of staff development, particularly for support staff whose training has often been neglected. His conclusions are that quality circles work best among 'natural' work groups, and need to be supported with resources such as consultant time, facilitator time and places to meet. He concludes his study with the words: 'Quality circles are not a panacea, but they can have dramatic results in terms of staff involvement, morale and identification with the aims of the organization. There are no disadvantages to introducing a quality circle programme, only varied levels of success' (Atkinson, 1990, p 89).

Chapter 10

Tools and Techniques for Quality Improvement

Educators should learn to use and interpret the basic strategies that are most frequently applied to quality improvement.
(Stanley J Spanbauer, *A Quality System for Education*, 1992, p 89)

Basic strategies and tools

There is a need to turn philosophy into practice and to develop practical means by which teams within education can achieve quality improvement. Quality tools and techniques are the means of identifying and creatively solving problems. One of the powerful aspects of TQM is the bringing together of a range of useful tools to implement its underlying concepts. However, the power of the tools can only be experienced by regular use. Most are simple and some, like brainstorming, are already in regular use. The important thing is to find the right tool for the job. Staff need to be trained in their proper use. There is often embarrassment in using such tools, but with practice they can become part of the decision-making culture of the institution.

Brainstorming

Brainstorming is an ideal TQM tool. It is also enjoyable and productive to use. It taps into the creativity of a team and allows them to generate ideas and issues quickly. A successful brainstorm allows staff to be inventive and free from restriction. However, it has limitations. While it excites the imagination and stimulates ideas, it is not a tool for analysis. Brainstorming does not provide objective assessments of a situation. As a result it needs to be used together with other tools, such as affinity networks or the construction of Ishikawa diagrams (see the next two sections). A team using brainstorming should follow some simple rules:

- Be clear what the brainstorming is about.
- Nominate someone to write the ideas down somewhere visible (a flipchart is ideal).
- List all ideas as they are expressed.
- Don't discuss or criticize ideas.
- Build on previous ideas.

A brainstorming session can be either a structured or an unstructured activity. Structured brainstorming involves every member of the team in turn giving ideas in rotation until the ideas run out. This forces everyone to take part and can be used to reinforce the identity of a team. Unstructured brainstorming simply allows people to express ideas as they come to mind. This method stimulates creativity, but it does enable the more vocal members to take control. Whichever method is used, a brainstorming session should never last for more than 10–15 minutes.

Affinity networks

This technique is used when there is the need to group a large number of ideas, opinions or issues and to categorize them. The aim is to identify which ideas have more affinity than others and to group them accordingly. The affinity network makes use of creative rather than logical processes. It helps make order out of chaos and stops a team drowning in a sea of ideas.

Affinity networks are a simple and powerful team process which starts with brainstorming. The team ideally should be kept small. The issue to be resolved needs clearly stating and must be understood by all. For example: 'what factors need considering in the student admission process? What issues are involved in unbiased advice and guidance?' The process that follows is a simple brainstorm with one difference. All the ideas are written on cards or Post-its. There should be no one-word ideas. There needs to be enough detail to provide clarity as to the meaning of any idea. At the end of the brainstorm the cards should be randomly laid out on a table, or if Post-its have been used they can be stuck on a whiteboard. This stage has one rule – it must be carried out in total silence. During the next stage the whole team sorts out the cards or Post-its into their related groupings. It is important to stress to the members in advance that this should be on the basis of their gut-reaction and should be a quick process. Everybody has the right to move all the cards in or out of a group and to create new ones. This might sound like a recipe for chaos but it is surprising how quickly a consensus develops. Once the groupings are established the team must quickly decide on a heading card or title for each grouping. They place the header cards at the top of their group. The header needs to capture the essential link between the ideas in each group.

The next stage is to work out the relationships or affinities between groupings by drawing lines to link them. This will produce a tree-diagram. The final result is a clarification of a complex set of issues or ideas into a small number of linked ideas with the relationship between them clearly established.

Fishbone or Ishikawa diagrams

This technique goes by a number of names including cause and effect, fishbone, or Ishikawa diagrams. The last-named is after Kaoru Ishikawa who first used them. The technique allows a team to map out all the factors which affect the problem or a desired outcome. The mapping may best be carried out through a brainstorming session. The aim is to list all the factors which affect the quality of a process and then to map the interrelationships between them.

The Ishikawa diagram is a visual list drawn up in a structured fashion. It illustrates the various causes affecting a process by sorting out and relating the causes to each other. For every effect there will be a number of causes and it is usual to group these in a number of major categories. This tool is used when an institution or a team needs to identify and explore the possible causes of a problem or look for the factors which could lead to an improvement.

Figure 10.1 *Ishikawa diagram*

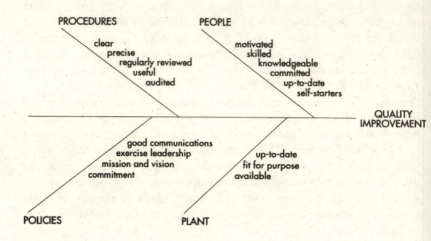

Force-field analysis

Force-field analysis is a useful tool for studying a situation which requires change. It is based on the idea that there are two opposing forces to change. One set of forces is driving the change while the other set resists. The analysis rests on the simple proposition that change can be brought about either by strengthening the promoting forces or neutralizing the resisting forces. It is a helpful tool because it promotes identification of all the forces which are involved. It is useful to remember that some of the resisting forces may be outside the institution's control and may not be worth while wasting time on. Effort should be spent on the areas it is possible to influence.

Process charting

This technique can be used to ensure that the institution knows who its customers are and can identify the resources required to service them.

Figure 10.2 *Force-field analysis*

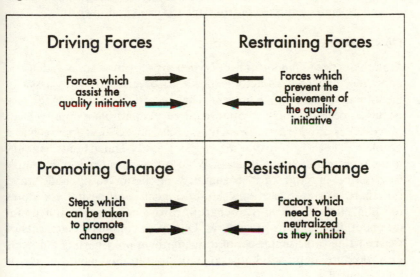

Figure 10.3 *Process charting*

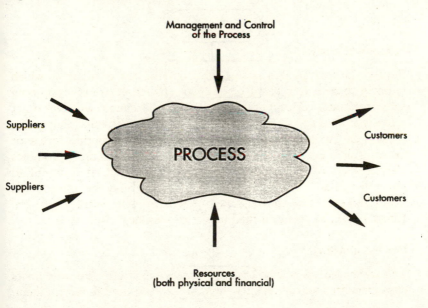

The process diagram provides data on the environment in which the process operates and the control which is exercised over it.

Flowcharts

Flowcharts are an important tool when a problem needs a systematic approach, or where an activity needs to be charted. They assist in identifying the steps in the process. They record the necessary sequence of stages, decisions and activities required. As part of an improvement process they provide a simple method of taking a critical approach to a problem. They also provide a clear and easily understood diagrammatic representation of a process. What often takes pages of narrative to describe in print can be summed up in an easily understood flowchart. For an educational establishment charting its procedures for BS5750 or ISO9000, flowcharting provides a simple and useful means of describing its procedures. One of the important elements of flowcharting is the simple act of drawing them up. Charting a process or procedure improves knowledge of it and highlights areas for improvement.

Figure 10.4 *Flowchart*

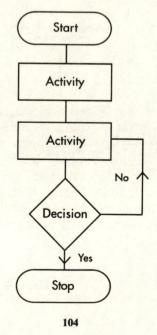

Figure 10.5 *Pareto chart*

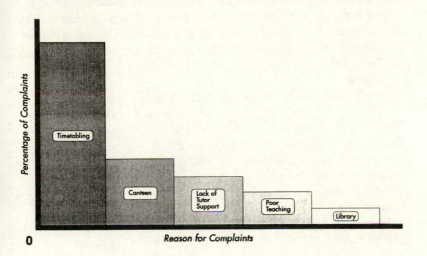

Pareto analysis

Pareto charts are named after the Italian economist Vilfredo Pareto, who at the end of the nineteenth century, while researching the distribution of wealth, came to the conclusion that the vast majority of wealth was in the hands of a tiny minority of the population. From this analysis has developed the famous Pareto Rule that 80 per cent of problems arise from 20 per cent of processes. Sometimes known as the 80/20 Rule, the Pareto Rule is an important idea. If the 80 per cent problem areas can be identified they should be tackled first in any quality improvement process. Effort should be put into the areas which cause the most difficulty. Pareto charts are simply special forms of vertical bar charts which assist in the solving of quality problems. Pareto charts direct attention to the most pressing problems facing a team or an institution.

Benchmarking

A benchmark is a standard against which to measure present

performance. It is usually undertaken by seeking the best of the competition and understanding the way they produce quality. In manufacturing, benchmarking is a powerful tool in new product development. It involves evaluating any new product against that of the industry leader. It can be taken a stage further so that not only the product, but also the systems used to produce the product are compared.

Benchmarking is the means of establishing a competitive advantage. It is about finding out who is the best and seeking to better it. Benchmarking provides a means of learning from and doing better than the market leader. It can considerably speed the development of a new curriculum and assure that quality standards are built in at the planning stage. The point of benchmarking is to ensure that your standards are at least as good if not better than those of your competitors.

In education there are various simple means of benchmarking which can be carried out as staff development exercises. Teachers can simply visit other institutions in their area and see how things are done. They can discover best practice and ensure that theirs matches it, and then seek to improve on it. The importance of benchmarking is that it saves reinvention. There is almost always someone somewhere who has solved your problem.

Career-path mapping

Charting a pupil's or student's career through the institution provides a simple means of identifying the milestones or the potential barriers which they will have to negotiate during their time at school or college. Each milestone is a potential problem area where differences in the perception and expectation have the possibility of leading to errors, misunderstandings, and possibly failure. A valuable exercise for an institution is to establish the learner's career-path and to identify against each milestone the quality characteristics and quality standards that should be in place.

When considering using this tool it is important to note that many of the problems and conflicts are likely to occur when the student or pupil passes from one stage to the next, rather than within each stage. While curriculum delivery is often seen as the most important stage in the learner's career there is a danger of focusing all the institution's attention on it at the expense of other career stages.

Chapter 11

Strategic Planning for Quality

If we accept that TQM is a long-term culture-change programme it must be planned for.

Planning for quality

Quality does not just happen. It must be planned for. Quality needs to be a major plank in an institution's strategy, and needs to be approached systematically using a rigorous strategic planning process. Strategic planning is one of the major planks of TQM. Without clear long-term direction the institution cannot plan for quality improvement. The first of Deming's 14 points is 'create constancy of purpose'. This can only be achieved within the context of a corporate strategy. Underlying the strategy must be the concept of strengthening the customer focus. A strong strategic vision is one of the most important critical success factors for any institution.

The process of strategic planning in education mirrors that normally followed in industry and commerce. The tools employed for establishing mission, goals and analysing strengths, weaknesses, opportunities and threats translate well. The tools themselves are simple and easy to apply. Their power results from the focus they give to the corporate thinking process. They force a questioning of why the institution exists, for whom it exists, and whether it is pursuing the right goals. These are important questions, particularly for institutions which have achieved independent corporate or grant-maintained status.

Strategic quality management

Strategic planning enables the formulation of long-term priorities, and it enables institutional change to be tackled in a rational manner. Without a strategy an institution cannot be certain that it is best placed to exploit new opportunities as they develop. The importance of undertaking the strategic exercise is not just to develop the corporate plan; useful as it is. The real significance is that it directs senior managers' attention away from day-to-day issues and forces a re-examination of the main purposes of the institution and its key

Figure 11.1 *The strategic planning process*

Mission and Vision
What is our purpose?
What are our vision, mission and values?

Customer/Learner Requirements
Who are our customers?
What do our customers expect of us?
What do we need to be good at to meet customer expectations?
What do our learners require from the institution?
What methods do we use to identify learner/customer needs?

Routes to Success
What are our strengths, weaknesses, opportunities and threats?
What factors are critical to our success?
How are we going to achieve success?

Quality Performance
What standards are we going to set?
How are we going to deliver quality?
What will quality cost us?

Investing in People
How should we make the most of our staff?
Are we investing sufficiently in staff and staff development?

Evaluating the Process
Do we have processes in place to deal with things that go wrong?
How will we know if we have been successful?

relationships with its customers. Figure 11.1 shows the key questions and issues that will be typically addressed by the strategic planning process.

There is no special sequence of activities when undertaking strategic planning, although it makes sense to move from the philosophical to the practical. However, it is important to take a systematic approach to planning the corporate future. Strategy must be based around the various customer groups and their expectations, and from these develop policies and plans which can deliver the mission and progress the vision. Figure 11.2 outlines a possible planning sequence which could be adopted by any educational institution.

Figure 11.2   *A possible planning sequence*

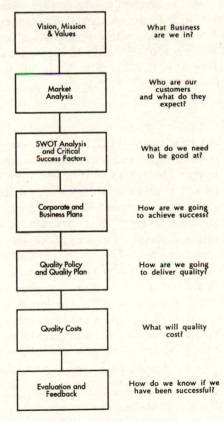

Vision, Mission & Values	What Business are we in?
Market Analysis	Who are our customers and what do they expect?
SWOT Analysis and Critical Success Factors	What do we need to be good at?
Corporate and Business Plans	How are we going to achieve success?
Quality Policy and Quality Plan	How are we going to deliver quality?
Quality Costs	What will quality cost?
Evaluation and Feedback	How do we know if we have been successful?

Vision, mission, values and goals

Many organizations make distinctions between their vision, mission, values, and goals (sometimes defined as aims and objectives). They do this to make it clear what sort of institution they wish to be and the direction they want it to move in.

The vision

The vision statement communicates the ultimate purpose of the institution and what it stands for. It needs to be short and direct and point out the ultimate purpose of the institution, for example: 'All our learners shall succeed'. Some commercial examples include, 'IBM means Service', or Disneyland's 'We create Happiness'. Some organizations start with these short and easy-to-remember bullet-points and then develop them with a further set of statements which flesh them out. For an educational institution something along the lines of 'Providing the Highest Standards of Learning' might constitute an appropriate vision statement.

The mission

The mission statement is closely linked to the vision, and provides a clear direction for the present and the future. The mission statement makes it clear why an institution is different from all the others. Mission statements are nowadays becoming well-established in education. What is not so prevalent is the strategic follow-through from mission to practical strategy. It is important to ensure that the mission is translated into necessary actions which are required to take advantage of the opportunities available to the institution.

Educational institutions are often reluctant to state publicly that they are seeking to become the best within their own particular sphere of operation. There is a fear that if the mission statement says this then the chances of failure are increased. However, if the mission statement is backed up by a well-formulated long-term quality strategy then this goal should be expressed in the mission statement. The following points should be borne in mind when drafting mission statements:

● They need to be memorable.

110

- They should be easy to communicate.
- The nature of the business should be made clear.
- There should be a commitment to quality improvement.
- They should be a statement of the long-term aims of the organization.
- They should be focused towards the customers.
- They should be flexible.

– 'Hightown School aims to provide its pupils with the highest possible quality of education.'
– 'Mid-County College of Arts and Technology aspires to be the leading provider of flexible quality academic and vocational programmes for school-leavers and adults in the county.'

Values

The values of an organization are the principles through which it operates and seeks to achieve the vision and its mission. They express the beliefs and aspirations of the institution. They should be short and crisp. Statements of values should be easy to remember and must be readily communicated throughout the institution. Values drive organizations and provide them with direction. They provide consistency of purpose. The values must be aligned to the environment in which the institution operates. They must strike a chord with both customers and staff. An institution must decide on its own values, but they could include many of the following:

- We put our learners first.
- We operate at the highest standards of professional integrity.
- We work as a team.
- We are committed to continuous improvement.
- We work to ensure equal opportunities for all.
- We will deliver the highest possible quality of service.

Goals

Once vision, mission, and values have been established they need to be translated into achievable goals. Goals are often expressed as aims and objectives. It is important that they are expressed in a measurable way so that the eventual outcomes can be evaluated against them. Goals must be realistic and achievable.

Market Research

Good market research is essential for implementing TQM. It is a prime means of listening to customers, both actual and potential. This may sound self-evident, but if a TQM approach is being contemplated then the customer-perceived notion of quality has to be established. The phrase 'perceived quality' is meaningless without market research. Research can be used to determine the issues as seen from the point of view of the customer. It can provide data on the image which the institution has with various different customer or potential customer groups. Institutions need to know what different groups think of them, and why some people use them and others do not. Different customer groups have distinctive needs and require diverse approaches and distinct forms of treatment. This form of sophisticated market discrimination is only possible if the institution has the evidence to hand.

Market research is not something that can be carried out once and for all time, especially in education. Education institutions have the interesting phenomenon of a population which moves through and out of the institution and is then replaced with a new cohort. There are repeat business possibilities, but education is different from most commercial activities as its core customers make a long-term commitment to it but rarely return for another sustained period of enrolment. In such a market, reputation is of vital importance. Reputations take time to develop and need to be guarded. They also change and market research can provide advance warnings of changes in customer perception of an institution.

The market analysis needs to take into account the segmentation of markets. Rarely does any organization operate in a single market. The different markets need to be identified. Once this has been achieved questions need to be asked about the distinctive requirements of each segment and whether the service needs to be customized to meet particular needs. This is particularly important in large further and higher education institutions where adult learners have different perceptions, needs and requirements from those of school-leavers. However, market segmentation analysis can be equally valid in schools. It is highly likely that different strategies will have to be adopted for each market segment if the perceived needs of the whole range of customers are to be met.

SWOT Analysis

SWOT analysis has become a commonplace tool of strategic planning in education, but it remains a most effective means of locating an institution's potential. The SWOT can be divided into two elements – an internal analysis concentrating on the performance of the institution itself, and an environmental analysis. The strengths and weaknesses exercise is essentially an internal audit of how effectively the institution performs. The threats and opportunities aspect concentrates on the external or environmental context in which the institution operates. The SWOT analysis aims to produce a small number of key areas under the headings: Strengths, Weaknesses, Opportunities and Threats. The aim of the exercise is to maximize strengths, minimize weaknesses, reduce threats and build on the opportunities.

The SWOT activity can be strengthened by ensuring that the analysis focuses on both the customer requirements, and the competitive context in which the institution operates. These are the two key variables in developing a long-term corporate strategy. The strategy of the institution needs to be developed in such ways that the institution can defend itself against the competition and can maximize its attractiveness to its customers. If this exercise is blended with the examination of the mission and values then a distinctive niche or identity can be sought which can differentiate the institution from its rivals. Once a distinctive identity can be developed it is considerably easier to identify the quality characteristics for an institution.

Moments of truth

Critical success factors (CSFs), sometimes called moments of truth, are the indicators of what must be achieved if an institution is to satisfy its customers and its mission statement. They are the next stage in the strategy process and provide a guide to the key quality characteristics of the institutions. They are similar, but not identical, to the more familiar performance indicators (PIs). The difference between CSFs and PIs is that the latter are often generated by others and are not always specifically related to the mission statement of the institution or its customer requirements. CSFs are the key activities

Figure 11.3 *SWOT analysis*

Strengths	Weaknesses
A strong enrolment	Old buildings in poor decorative condition
Enthusiastic management team	High average age of staff
Excellent examination results	Inadequate budget
Strong music, art & drama departments	Lack of car parking
Strong parental support	Inadequate sports facilities
Good staff morale	
Supportive Governors	

Opportunities	Threats
Merger with local institution with an excellent site but mediocre reputation	Loss of identity, strengths and reputation
Develop reputation in sport	Risk of losing experienced teachers who may take early retirement
The excitement of establishing a new institution	
The opportunity to enlarge staff expertise in order to increase the range of offerings	That the ethos of the other institution may become dominant
The merged institution may attract additional funding	Possible loss of some supportive Governors

which the institution identifies for itself. A list of an institution's critical success factors could include external measures such as customer satisfaction or responsiveness to community needs, as well as internal indicators such as the amount of staff professional updating, or the successful operation of teams. The key to listing CSFs is to concentrate on the words 'critical' and 'success'. CSFs must highlight what has to be achieved if the institution is to move to total quality. Internal critical success factors might include:

- An accessible admissions system.
- Learning modes which meet learner needs.
- Properly functioning teams.
- Improved examination pass rates.
- Learner development of social, personal, cultural and ethical values.
- Improvements in teaching/learning strategies.
- Involvement of the majority of staff in improvement teams.
- Improved progression rates, eg into employment and further and higher education.

The external critical success factors could include:

- Improved access to the institution.
- Greater customer satisfaction evidenced through surveys.
- Increased market share.
- Increased take up of provision by minority and disadvantaged groups.
- Greater responsiveness to community needs.
- Stronger relationship with industry and commerce.

The strategic plan

The strategic plan, sometimes called a corporate or institutional development plan, details the measures which the institution intends to take to achieve its mission. It sets a medium-term time-scale, usually over a three-year period. Its aim is to give the institution guidance and direction. However, the plan is not a rigid instrument and should be modified if significant internal or external events require it. In a competitive market for education the production of a strategic plan assumes considerable importance. Without it the institution lacks direction.

The strategic plan needs to address a number of key issues once the analysis of mission, values, SWOT and critical success factors has been undertaken. Any institution must decide on:

Market identification. This may be decided for it, but whether this is the case or whether new markets can be opened, the nature of the market provides the essential setting for the strategic plan.

The degree of market penetration the institution expects to make. Any institution must have a target for the degree of market share it is seeking to achieve.

Its portfolio of services. This must link closely with market identification and market penetration. Without the appropriate portfolio of courses and programmes it is impossible to meet stated goals.

The development of the portfolio. If the institution is lacking the programmes geared to its targeted markets then it clearly needs a strategy and time-scale to develop them. The development will not only include new programmes but also new and flexible means of delivering existing programmes.

Developing long-term institutional strategies

There are a number of generic strategies which organizations can adopt once they have decided which services and which markets they are operating in. There is a choice of three generic marketing strategies which any institution can follow (see Christopher, Payne and Ballantyne, 1991, pp 52–4). The first is *cost-leadership strategy*. This requires an organization to be the lowest cost institution within its market. It may seek to do this by the extensive use of technology, economies of scale, strict control of costs, etc. The benefits of this strategy are that it can target resources to the areas identified as critical to the customers' perception of quality. However, being the cheapest does not by itself guarantee success. Many consumers will pay more for quality. Quality must not be sacrificed in the drive to reduce unit costs. Within those areas of education where the service is provided free this strategy does not appear relevant at first sight. However, a school which, for example, is able to control its costs or employ economies of scale will have additional sums of money to employ as it wishes. The results of the effective deployment of its resources can provide it with a competitive edge.

The second, *differentiation*, is a strategy which requires an institution to be unique in some way from its competitors. In a commercial market this may allow the company to charge a premium price. Within education the gains are largely in terms of being able to attract additional pupils or students, and the unique features may make it easier to attract alternative sources of funding. An obvious form of differentiation is the opportunity for schools to specialize as outlined in the 1992 White Paper, *Choice and Diversity*. Quality is important for any institution which may wish to exploit this strategy because institutions claiming uniqueness will be subject to close scrutiny.

The third possible market strategy is called *focus strategy*. This involves concentrating on a particular geographical area, a customer group, or a market segment. It is a strategy of differentiation through market segmentation. By targeting, the institution will aim to tailor its programmes closer to the needs of the targeted groups than those of its rivals. As with all strategies the aim is to gain a competitive advantage. The cost of doing this is to give up operating across the whole market range. Again, quality is equally necessary for this strategy. Targeting will only work if the quality meets the customers' needs.

Business and operating plans

The business or operating plan is the short-term, usually one-year, detailed plan for achieving particular aspects of the institution's longer-term corporate strategy. It contains definite measures and the financial implications of putting them into operation. As well as the direct financial benefits and costs it should include the non-financial benefits such as enhanced reputation, increased profile, etc.

The quality policy and the quality plan

It is important for an institution to have a clear statement of policy on quality. The quality policy is a statement of commitment by the institution. If an institution is following the BS5750/ISO9000 route it

Figure 11.4 *Questions to be asked in drawing up a business or operating plan*

- Is there a clear definition of the service being offered?
- Is there a clear strategy to produce the service to specification?
- Have all the external customers been identified?
- Is there a clear definition of external customers' needs?
- Are there gaps between the expectations of customers and the current specification of the service?
- Can any gaps between expectation and specifications be closed?
- Are the expectations of customers incorporated as fully as possible in the service specification?
- Have the suppliers been identified?
- Have the suppliers been as fully informed as possible about requirements?
- Are there gaps between supply and requirements?
- How are gaps between supply and requirements being closed?
- Have all the resource requirements been identified?
- Are the resources adequate to meet the specification?
- Are there gaps between the needs of the specification and the available resources?
- Can gaps in resource requirements be closed?
- Have the training needs of the staff been identified?
- Does the process to be used produce the service to the specification?
- Does the process meet the expectations of the customers?
- Have we defined what a successful outcome is?
- Have the critical success factors been identified for the process?
- Are there adequate monitoring mechanisms in place to measure success?
- Are there adequate feedback mechanisms in place to allow for self-checking and self-evaluation?

is a requirement. However, it is useful for all institutions to draw one up as it is a practical way for them to define their own quality. A good example of a quality policy is that of Fox Valley Technical College in Wisconsin which states that:

QUALITY FIRST POLICY

It is the policy of Fox Valley Technical College to provide quality instruction and service consistent with the highest educational standards.

We endeavour to provide precise, prompt and courteous service and instructions to our students, to one another, and to the employers who hire our graduates and use our services (Fox Valley, 1991, p iii).

The next stage is to develop the quality plan. The quality plan puts the quality policy statement into action. It shows how the process of quality improvement is to be made and maintained. Clearly, it must relate closely both to the corporate and business plans but its focus is different. It outlines the processes to be taken in the medium term to deliver quality improvements. As a result the quality plan must have clear aims and objectives in relation to quality and the methods through which management commitment is translated into action. Additionally, it must detail the mechanisms through which staff can participate in quality improvement teams. The quality plan should detail the improvement projects which the college intends to carry out. This is the document in which the grand design and the large-scale aspirations are turned into practical and manageable projects.

The costs and benefits of quality

Quality costing is about measuring the benefits of quality improvement. TQM should be approached from the standpoint that it will bring measurable benefits to the institution. Good ideas have to be measured, costed and evaluated. The effort to undertake TQM is considerable in human and financial terms and the benefits flowing from it have to be shown to provide a payback. Any improvement project should be approached with the expectation that it will bestow benefits which exceed the costs of it.

Another way of appreciating the gains from TQM is to measure the cost of things going wrong – known as the costs of failure or nonconformance. Frustrated customers, inefficient or ineffective ways of doing things, and simple mistakes cost the institution. The costs can be generated from a number of sources – angry parents, lost enrolments, extra work, lost income, wasted staff effort. The TQM approach is to try to make things right first time every time and to aim for zero defects. Complaints must be taken seriously and rectified. The feedback loop is important. There must be a system which takes up complaints and looks into serious mistakes and ensures that the loophole which created them does not occur a second time.

'Right first time' is a difficult concept to implement in a human activity like education. It is not always possible to achieve but every institution should always aim to get it right the second time around. Making honest mistakes, however, should not be seen as a matter for blame. Honest mistakes can be the result of innovation and initiative, and excessive caution can be a double-edged sword. The important thing is to minimize mistakes with clear systems and procedures, and good teamwork. Careful and thoughtful planning is an important means of getting things right first time. The test of a TQM organization is how well it responds to mistakes, ensures that they do not recur, and learns the lessons for its future operation. Recurring errors and mistakes demonstrate a lack of system and ineffective or inoperative methods of feedback.

The costs of prevention and failure

There are various ways of measuring quality costs, but an essential distinction can be drawn between the costs of prevention and the costs of failure. The costs of prevention are essentially those costs required to stop things going wrong and to ensure that things are done properly. Under this heading are the costs of quality improvement, the setting up of quality systems, the salaries of co-ordinators and quality managers, training, and supporting teamwork. These costs are direct costs and can be readily quantified.

The costs of failure, or non conformance as it is called in the literature on quality, are often more difficult to measure and are usually opportunity costs, which are measured via lost opportunities and lost business. Included in these costs are customer dissatisfaction, lost enrolments, learner failure, reworking and redoing things which should have been done correctly first time, time wasting and frustration. The failure costs are all the things that take the pleasure out of managing and working in education. The real cost of quality is eliminating non-quality. The aim of quality costing is zero costs. That is to say ensuring that things are always done correctly. If things do go wrong it is essential to establish root cause of the failure so that the same thing can be prevented from happening again.

Figure 11.5 *Quality costs*

Prevention costs	Failure costs
Internal	*Internal*
TQM development	Dissatisfied learners
Staff training	Poor teaching/learning strategies
Effective teamwork	Poor examination/test results
Effective quality system	Poorly motivated staff
Strategic plan	Poor administrative systems
Audit and evaluation	Inadequate learner support
External	*External*
Effective employer, parent and community liaison	Complaints
	Switchboard problems
Appraisal of customer satisfaction	Poor publicity
	Declining reputation

Monitoring and evaluation

Quality systems always need a feedback loop. Mechanisms must be in place to ensure that outcomes can be analysed against the plan. Monitoring and evaluation are key elements in strategic planning. If the institution is to be a learning rather than a static organization a process of evaluation and feedback must be an essential element in its culture. The evaluation process should focus on the customer, and explore two issues: first, the degree to which the institution is meeting the individual requirements of its customers, both internal and external; and second, how far it is achieving its strategic mission and goals. To ensure that evaluation is monitoring both individual and institutional goals it must take place at three levels:

Immediate – involving the daily checking of pupil/student progress. This type of evaluation is largely informal in nature, and is undertaken by individual teachers or at the team level.

Short-term – requiring more structured and specific means of evaluation, which ensures that pupils/students are on track and are achieving their potential. Its purpose is to make certain that things that need to be put right are corrected. The use of statistical data and student profiling should be features of this process. It is undertaken at a team and departmental level. Short-term evaluation can be employed as a method of quality control to highlight mistakes and problems. The emphasis is on corrective action to prevent, so far as is practical, pupil/student failure or under-achievement.

Long-term – an overview of the progress towards achieving strategic goals. This is mainly institutional-led evaluation. It requires large-scale sampling of customer attitudes and views, as well as monitoring by a range of institutional performance indicators. This type of evaluation is undertaken as a prelude to updating the strategic plan. It can involve the use of questionnaires to gain feedback from both primary and secondary customers. The information gained from surveys can be cross-referenced with quantitative performance data on successes, pass rates, student destinations, etc. An important purpose of this type of evaluation is prevention. Finding out what has gone wrong, and what pupils/students have not benefited from, and then preventing it from happening again. It is a checking mechanism to ensure that continuous improvement initiatives are meeting their objectives. An interesting model of using student feedback as a means of strategic institutional review can be found in A Roberts' innovative paper *Establishing Customer Needs and Perception*, which compares the priorities established by a college with those of its primary customers and its parents and employers. What Roberts found is that the priorities of his students varied in a number of significant ways from those established through the usual management mechanisms. It also highlighted the things which were of most importance to his parent groups, which were termly reports, parents' evenings, and contacts with staff (see Roberts, 1992).

The function of evaluation at each stage is different. Too often evaluation is seen as having *prevention* as its main purpose. It is a means of discovering what went right and wrong and using the information to improve things next time round, which in education usually means next year. Preventing things from happening again is a perfectly valid use of evaluation, but it has a major drawback. It does not put right the things that have gone wrong for this year's pupils and students. If problems are identified there must be mechanisms to correct them immediately. Pupils and students should not be allowed to suffer. Putting things right next year will not help them. They need *corrective* action to improve their learning or to stop them under-achieving or failing. A primary purpose of evaluation is to ensure that students are on target, and if they are not, to take the necessary actions to guarantee that they reach their goals. Unfortunately, evaluation is too often used to improve future rather than present provision.

The failure to distinguish the long term from the short term has led to evaluation mechanisms being employed in possibly misleading ways. Too much emphasis in formal evaluation is on prevention rather than correction. In further education, for example, the main evaluation paradigm bases evaluation around elaborate, periodic, often termly, student questionnaires. The aim is to establish close student feedback and to establish the validity of the curriculum delivery processes, as well as to seek out student perceptions of the college's services. There is nothing intrinsically wrong with questionnaires or with this type of evaluation, providing it is clear what value the output has. This type of evaluation is excellent for identifying strategic and institutional issues. It is far less effective as a method of identifying the factors which have affected the performance of individual students.

Questionnaires are of most value for identifying macro-issues – access to the institution, equal opportunities, perception of the refectory, general teaching styles, etc – rather than for identifying the micro-issues which affect individual performance – feedback on the last assignment, whether the student is achieving what has been agreed in their action plan, or whether they have difficulties in a particular subject. It is not possible to check on an individual student's learning by periodically analysing the results of questionnaires. An individual's perceptions and problems become lost in aggregate scores for the group. This danger is heightened when questionnaires are drawn up to reflect the institution's priorities and concerns rather than those of the students. Only very occasionally are questionnaires drawn up after a full analysis of what is important to students. This is not to argue that customer surveys are not of value. They are of tremendous value for marketing and strategic planning. However, to gain this type of information they need only to be administered periodically on a sample basis. It is important not to confuse the preventative and long-term improvement purposes of evaluation and neglect the simpler forms of evaluation which can provide possible immediate solutions to particular problems. Checking on individual performance can better be based around action planning and the charting of student progress, and around well-thought-out and planned tutorial programmes than through highly elaborate processes.

Chapter 12

Conclusion – Implementing TQM

Quality is about customer delight rather than customer satisfaction. It is about total staff involvement rather than hierarchical, top-down system imposition. It is about incremental quality improvement rather than giant quality leaps. It is about living, loving, passion, fighting, cherishing, nurturing, struggling, crying, laughing...
(Tony Henry, Principal East Birmingham College, quoted in Sallis and Hingley, *Total Quality Management*, 1992, p 65).

Effective institutions need strong and purposeful strategies to deal with the competitive and results-orientated climate of the 1990s. To be effective in this climate institutions require processes for developing their quality strategy. These include:

- a clear and distinctive mission;
- a clear customer focus;
- a strategy for achieving that mission;
- the involvement all of their customers, both internal and external, in the development of strategy;
- the empowerment of staff by removing barriers and assisting them to make the maximum contribution to the institution through the development of effective work groups;
- the assessment and evaluation the institution's effectiveness against the goals negotiated with customers.

Institutions which decide to travel this road can become so overwhelmed by the seeming enormity of the task and the wealth and diversity of advice that there is a danger of 'total quality paralysis' overtaking them. Deciding when and where to start on total quality is a very difficult task. Perhaps the only task more difficult is having the will to continue, especially after the inevitable setbacks. There is no magic formula for starting the task, although there are a number of simple and important steps which can be followed:

Leadership and commitment to quality must come from the top – the 'iron law' of quality. All models of quality emphasize that without the drive of senior management quality initiatives will be short-lived. Education is no exception to this iron law. 'Unless the chief school officer leads the way, the concept is doomed to failure. Middle-level managers alone cannot ensure success. The school head must demonstrate strong and sustained commitment and lead the way while encouraging principals, vice-principals, and other supervisors to take the effort seriously' (Spanbauer, 1992, p 8).

Delighting the customers is the purpose of TQM. This is achieved by a continual striving to meet both internal and external customers' needs and expectations. Customers' needs are established by regularly soliciting their views. There are various methods of doing this – focus groups, questionnaires, advisory groups, open days, and informally talking to people. It is important that this work is done systematically, and that the views of people who decide not to attend the institution are also solicited. The information from these consultations must be collated and analysed and used when taking decisions. It is important to involve the customers in the process because at the end of the day it is their views that count not those of the institution's management. As Mike Barrett and Marion Thorpe have so aptly expressed it: 'Students do not come to the college because there is a great budget or good SSRs; to them quality is about convenience, promptness, courtesy and reliability ...' (Sallis and Hingley, 1992, p 62).

Designating a quality champion or facilitator. Regardless of the actual position of this person in the hierarchy it is important that the designated quality facilitator should report directly to the Headteacher or Principal. It is the responsibility of the facilitator to publicize the programme, and to lead the quality steering group in developing the quality programme.

Forming a quality steering group. This group must represent key interests and must have representation from the senior management team. Its role is to drive and support the quality improvement process. It is both the powerhouse of ideas and the initiator of projects.

Appointing quality co-ordinators. It is useful in any initiative to have people who have the time to coach and mentor others. The coordinators do not undertake all the quality projects. Their role is to assist and guide teams in discovering new ways to tackle and solve problems.

Holding senior management seminars to evaluate progress. The senior management team will not be committed to the process unless they are well informed about both the philosophy and the methods. It is necessary to build up a well-integrated and robust senior management team. They need to set an example to the teams in the rest of the institution. If TQM requires a 180 degree turn this can only happen if the senior managers are as well trained as anyone else in the institution, and are prepared to change their working patterns to support the development of new ways of working. Specific training in strategic approaches to quality will probably be necessary. The senior management team must lead the quality cascade.

Analysing and diagnosing the present situation. The means of doing this has been thoroughly covered in Chapter 11 on Strategic Planning for Quality. Its importance should not be underestimated because it provides the direction for the whole process. All institutions need to be clear about where they are and where they are going.

Using models developed elsewhere. This could be an adaptation of the work of one of the quality 'gurus', a specifically educational model, or one that a local company is adopting. While other people's models rarely fit, the process of researching them is usually helpful to clarifying thinking. Many industrial companies are willing to share their approaches.

Employing external consultants. This is a very popular starting point for industrial companies, especially those who are implementing BS5750 or ISO9000. This is unlikely to be a popular route for education as consultancy is expensive and grants from the Department of Trade and Industry are not available to education. However, many institutions with industrial partners may find that these are prepared to advise without charge. There are inherent dangers in using consultants. They can be useful in giving advice and asking the awkward questions, but they must never be allowed to drive the process. Over reliance on external consultants has been a cause of many TQM failures in industry. Institutions need to learn to develop quality for themselves. If a consultant is used it is important to select one whose ideas and approaches match those of the institution, and who has a 'feel' for what it is trying to achieve.

Consultants can be used in one of four main ways. First, they can provide initial advice and guidance and 'convert' the senior management team. Firing the team with enthusiasm can be an important role which consultants can usefully fulfil. The second role is in training. Money will need to be put aside for training. Skilled external trainers can achieve a great deal in terms of awareness-raising and instruction in tools and techniques. Third, consultants can be powerful 'irritants' when brought in to ask difficult questions. Fourth, consultants can be useful in carrying out formal audits, assessments and evaluation.

Initiating staff training for quality. Staff development can be seen as an essential tool for building the awareness and knowledge of quality. It can be the key strategic change agent for developing the quality culture. If TQM is largely about culture then a means has to be found of capturing the hearts and minds of staff. It has long been recognized by motivational theorists that training is one of the most important motivators in an organization's armoury.

It is important in the initial stages of implementation that everyone is trained in the basics of TQM. Staff need a knowledge of some of the key tools including teamwork, evaluation methods, problem-solving and decision-making techniques. Both internal and external trainers have their part to play. It can be helpful to visit other organizations, whether educational or business, which are developing total quality initiatives.

Having analysed the success of a number of major US companies, Tom Peters, in *Thriving on Chaos*, comes up with the exhortation, 'Train Everyone – Lavishly'. Peters provides a prescription for what constitutes a successful organizational training programme. Training should be used as the flagship for strategic change. Peters argues that management in the future will flow through empowering visions and shared values. Training is a prime opportunity to underscore the organization's values. To do this top management must be closely involved in training programmes (see Peters, 1987, pp 324–8).

Communicating the quality message. The strategy, relevance and benefits of TQM need to be effectively communicated. There can be a great deal of misunderstanding about the purpose of quality. The long-term nature of the programme needs to be made clear, as do the reasons for embarking on it. Staff development, training and team building are some of the most effective means of achieving it. Staff need to be regularly informed with either special newsletters or regular reports in the in-house journal. The importance of good communications and their feedback to management cannot be overemphasized. It is important to highlight good practices so that positive attitudes and goodwill can be drawn on. An institution will need to find its champions and leaders and to recognize their successes. Achievement needs to be celebrated, and there needs to be public recognition of good work. This does not have to be monetary recognition, but the motivational effects of public recognition and praise should not be underestimated. All the staff need to be involved in the quality process. The quality system needs to be the institution's own. The importance of staff ownership of the quality improvement process cannot be overstated.

Measuring the costs of quality. It is important to know both the cost of implementing the quality programme and the costs of not undertaking it. The costs of ignoring the quality message could involve lost enrolments, student failures, damage to reputation, lost opportunities, etc. The exercise is important as it highlights many of the reasons for pursuing quality improvements and provides a motivation for sticking with the programme.

Applying quality tools and techniques through the development of effective work groups. This approach focuses on getting things done and achieving initial successes. It focuses on the things that the institution knows it has to improve, and selecting the correct tools to tackle them. Starting a TQM process by tackling problems head on avoids TQM paralysis. The danger with it, as an approach, is that it is easy to run out of steam or for the initiative to flounder if problems are difficult to resolve. If this approach is adopted it needs, to be closely followed by a thorough analysis and a more strategic approach. Nevertheless, it may be useful to demonstrate those important first achievements.

Projects are best tackled by teams, and they should be encouraged to tackle problems and issues close to home. Tom Peters believes that organizations should 'encourage pilots for everything' (Peters, 1987, p 221). Pilots have the advantage of speeding up innovation, providing sources of excitement and interest. When setting up improvement action teams or task groups it is important to recognize that some issues can only be tackled by cross-organizational improvement teams. These are probably best set up as *ad hoc* groups, given the brief to tackle a particular problem according to a fixed time-scale. They have the additional advantage of helping to engender greater organizational collaboration.

Teams can start by analysing work flows and the existing processes and methods and their results. Usually the process of analysis highlights areas which need improvement and provides the initial

Figure 12.1 *The quality circle*

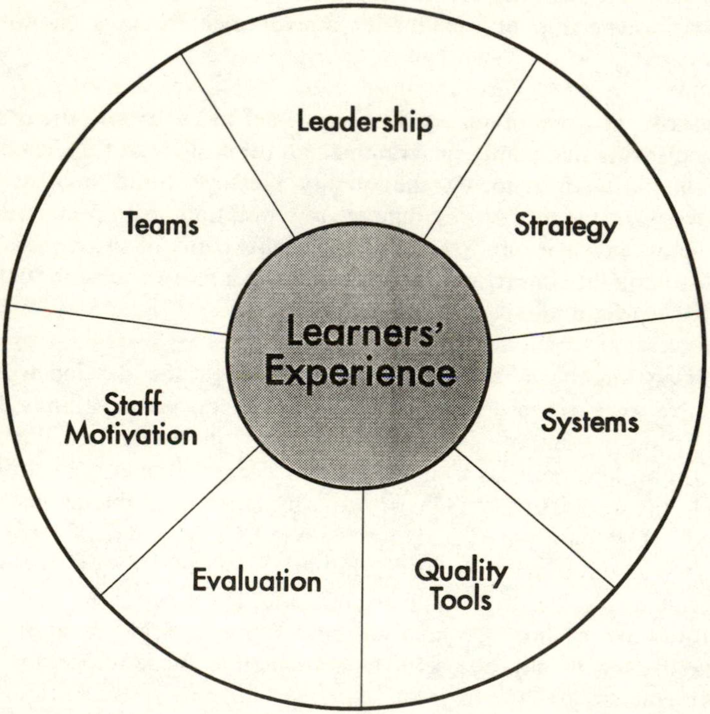

agenda for the improvement programme. It is important that teams be supported with training in teamwork, problem-solving and the use of tools if they are be successful in their task.

Evaluating the programme at regular intervals. There is a danger of TQM programmes running out of steam or becoming derailed. Regular review and evaluation needs to be an integral part of the programme. The steering group should undertake regular six-monthly reviews and the senior management team should consider their reports and carry out its own monitoring. No new initiatives should be undertaken until the successes and failures of the existing ones are fully understood.

Designing your own quality system

An institution may decide to start its TQM initiative with BS5750 or ISO9000, but even if it decides not to follow this route, it may nevertheless wish to devise a quality system to assure the quality of its service delivery. This will allow it to define and monitor its own systems and procedures against a set of defined measures and standards. While there is no 'kitemark', neither is there the expense of conforming to someone else's standard or the cost of external assessment. To proceed along this route an institution will need to define its own standards for the principal attributes of quality, and it will also need to set up arrangements for achieving them. An institution's own system need not be bureaucratic or heavily paper-based, although it will involve a certain amount of paperwork, which is necessary to provide the evidence required. A quality system involves a number of important steps:

- discovering what you are doing;
- questioning your methods and procedures;
- documenting what you intend to do;
- doing what you say you are doing;
- providing evidence that you are accomplishing what you are claiming to be doing. This enables the information to be shared with everyone else.

A quality system of the type outlined below could be, if thoroughly developed, converted to one capable of being BS5750/ISO9000 accredited if the institution subsequently desired it. An educational quality assurance system should contain the following elements:

Institutional development or strategic plan

This provides the long-term vision of the institution and gives the context in which its programmes operate. It defines markets and the desired culture. It is essential for delivering a quality service because only planning can provide the long-term perspective so important in the delivery of a total quality service.

Quality policy

This lays out the standards for the main programmes and may contain a statement of the entitlements of learners. The policy is a public statement of the commitment of the institution to its customers, both internal and external.

Management responsibility

This lays out the role of the governing body, and the senior management team and their responsibilities. It defines which member of the senior team carries the quality portfolio.

The quality organization

This outlines the scope of the responsibility of the quality steering group, its representation and accountability. This body is needed to steer the quality initiative, manage the cultural transformation, oversee and support the initiatives in departments, and to monitor the progress of initiatives.

The function of teams both to run programmes and to solve problems is a main building block of the quality initiative. The support, leadership and resources, and the training available to teams needs to catalogued.

Marketing and publicity

An institution should provide its potential customers with clear information about what it is offering in its programmes of learning. This information needs to be clearly documented and available. The marketing material – prospectus, leaflets, brochures, etc, must be clear and accurate and regularly updated.

Inquiries and admissions

This is a key stage in the career of any learner. The right advice at this stage is vital, as is the welcome and care given to applicants. The institution's entry procedures must be well documented and regularly reviewed. The systems which need to be documented include: initial application, interview and selection, guidance, enrolment, the accreditation of prior learning where appropriate, and the production of individual action plans.

Induction

A well-structured pupil/student induction programme with clearly communicated aims is important to introduce learners to the institution, its ethos and the styles and methods of learning. The induction needs to be subject to evaluation to ensure that the needs of learners have been met.

The delivery of the curriculum

This is the stage where systems are vital. The methods of learning need to be established and followed for each aspect of the programme. The type of information which needs to be part of it includes: syllabuses, course submissions, schemes of work, records of work, assessment records, action plans, and records of achievement. The recording of failure and below average performance and the actions taken to correct them should be documented.

Equally the systems which the institution has developed to assist those with learning difficulties require recording. The details of both formative and summative assessments and the criteria for grading and the award of qualifications are necessary elements of the quality system. Details of appeals procedures, if relevant, should be included.

Guidance and counselling before exit

This can take the form of an integrated aspect of the curriculum or an additional service. Whichever it is, the service needs to be defined and communicated. This may be guidance on careers or further and higher education, or transfer to another institution or programme of study.

The management of learning

The actual process of curriculum and programme management needs to be specified, including arrangements for teamwork. The roles within the team and their responsibilities and levels of authority also can be spelt out. The reports of external examiners, moderators and verifiers will provide important evidence, where available, of the quality of the management of learning.

Curriculum design

This includes documentation of the aims and objectives of each programme, and the specification of the programme. The latter can take the form of a syllabus or submission document to a validating body. What needs to be included, where relevant, is the evidence for the demand for the programme and the resources devoted to it. Evidence of learners' or sponsors' inputs into the design will be a feature of this part of the quality system.

Staffing, training and development

The staff of any institution need to be seen to be competent to carry out their tasks. The quality system will need to detail the staff selection and recruitment process, induction, and the means by which competence and motivation are assessed, as well as the policies for career development.

Staff development requires both an institutional plan and a process of needs analysis, as well as the systems for monitoring and evaluating the effectiveness of training programmes both in the short and the long-run. The criteria of the Investors in People standard can be used as a checklist to determine the standards that need to be met in this area.

Equal opportunities

The institution will need to detail both its equal opportunities policy and the methods and procedures it uses to achieve the aims contained in the policy. The equal opportunities policy needs to be equally applicable to staff and pupils/students.

Monitoring and evaluation

Feedback loops are vital for assessing and assuring quality. The quality system will need to document the evaluation mechanisms that the institution has in place to monitor both the achievement of individuals and the success of its programmes. The participation of the learners in the assessment of their own progress and their experience of the programme is an important element in this assessment. The methods might include records of achievement, review meetings, questionnaires, and internal audits. Whatever the method employed they must be appropriate to the process.

Administrative arrangements

The institution will need to document its main administrative procedures including enrolment, learners' records, timetables, health and safety procedures, examination entries and results, and financial systems. The process of document control is important, although it is necessary to specify the key documents and their status in order to prevent the development of a considerable paper-based bureaucracy. Key documents will include up-to-date copies of syllabuses, approval and validation documents, course and student records, assessment and testing records, key committee minutes, etc.

Institutional review

An institution should have a means of evaluating its total performance. This may be undertaken by external inspectors. However, the institution may decide to undertake its own audit. Staff can assess areas other than their own. Outsiders may be included in the audit. A system of peer review can build confidence and trust, and can act as significant staff development. Mechanisms need to be developed to feed the results of this auditing back into the strategic planning processes.

Some final thoughts

TQM fits well into the general philosophy, although less frequently into the practice, of education. The ideas of client-centredness, which are at the heart of the total quality approach, are in tune with much educational philosophy. All institutions claim to be pupil- or student-centred. The difference between this aspiration and a total quality institution is that of a comprehensive framework to assure that promises are delivered to customers. The gaps between intention and assuring quality arise, in part, because educational institutions have, in general, been excellent in responding to external change, but have often lacked the time and the mental resources to plan their own long-term strategy and develop their own standards. A total quality approach, whether the initials TQM are adopted or not, will be necessary for the future corporate health and survival of institutions. A clear identity, well-defined standards and customer entitlements are necessary features of self-confident institutions. Institutions will need to find the time to plan for their own and their customers' future.

They will need to produce a coherent and integrated approach to quality management which harnesses the commitment and goodwill of staff. Motivation, expertise and enthusiasm assure quality, not appraisal and inspection. The quality improvement programme must involve all who work in the institution. Everybody is responsible for the quality of the service they deliver whether they are institutional managers, teachers or staff in support roles. Harnessing commitment from staff and channelling it into improvements is a major aspect of TQM. Quality systems must be vehicles for assisting staff to solve their own problems, not means of controlling them. It is all too easy to turn a quality system into a means of control rather than of empowerment. It is important to remember that people produce quality, and to ensure that there are practical means of recognizing their achievements. Educationalists need to keep in mind that the quality message is in essence extremely simple. Quality is about doing the ordinary things extraordinarily well.

No institution can purchase TQM off the peg. It has to be customized so that it harmonizes with and develops from the existing culture. TQM should be developed from existing good practice within the institution. Quality already exists in educational institutions. What TQM does is to build on existing quality and develop it into continuous quality improvement. Industrial models can be drawn on to provide useful pointers and examples. However, it is important to ensure that any approach used is realistic, workable and affordable. It needs to be remembered that introducing total quality requires perseverance. TQM is not something which can be introduced overnight. Nor is it a miracle cure. It does not provide instant success, and it does not solve all the problems. It will throw up new difficulties and challenges. It is a slow process and the benefits are long-term. No institution has to adopt the message of total quality. However, let us not forget that in the current climate no institution, however long established, has an automatic right to survival.

Appendix: Measuring Up – a Self-assessment Checklist

The use of a self-diagnosis or quality-audit instrument is an excellent first step on the path to total quality. The audit checklist is a standard against which the institution can measure itself. It provides a framework for building up a definition of quality, it helps the institution decide where they are now in relation to current thinking on the quality of provision and it allows them to build an action plan for development. It can also usefully be employed at intervals to measure progress and to evaluate success and failure. There are a range of self-assessment tools available, including the elaborate audit document produced for further education colleges by the Further Education Unit, *Towards An Educational Audit* (FEU 1989). Another useful checklist is part of the 'Investors In People' toolkit available from Training and Enterprise Councils: *How Do We MEASURE UP?* (Department of Employment, 1991).

The problem with many quality-audit checklists is that they appear daunting. By listing all the possible criteria for excellence they create an aura of perfection which can appear impossible to achieve. The following checklist has been devised as a simple tool. It covers the essentials and concentrates on the areas of greatest importance to the customers. The checklist is flexible in its scope and purpose: not all institutions will necessarily agree with all of the values or priorities which are implicit in it. Institutions can modify it or use it as the basis for devising their own. It is an instrument for aiding policy and decision-making.

Using the checklist

The usual way of using a checklist is for the senior management team of an institution to score their perceptions of how the institution measures up. There is nothing wrong with this, but it should also be used with the staff and, at the least, with a representative sample of differing customer groups. The different perceptions of the different groups can be extremely revealing. It can also lead to a changing in the order of an institution's strategic priorities.

Another way of using such an instrument is to set up an audit team with the job of collecting the evidence to support the conclusions drawn from each item. Part of the evidence-collecting procedure would be contact with staff and students through the use of focus groups. The audit team should ideally be a mixed group involving senior management, teaching and support staff, students and possibly an external customer such as an employer's representative. The team could then report back to the appropriate decision-making committees within the institution. The importance of such an audit approach is that the actual process of collecting the evidence is both a developmental and evaluative exercise. It is important to recognize that this type of quality auditing is developmental rather than judgemental in character. It is not about finding faults but about highlighting good practice and showing areas where development and change will bring benefits. It is a guide to improvement and planning.

The quality education checklist

Score 1 for poor performance and 5 for excellence.

	1	2	3	4	5

Access

Point of contact
- Clear initial contact point for customers
- Welcoming reception
- Short telephone response time
- Advice and guidance readily available

	1	2	3	4	5

- Survey of how well visitors think they were received
- clear signing on the site

Open access
- Ramps and lifts for people with disabilities
- Community languages on signs and in literature

Services for customers

Advice and guidance
- Information and guidance service available
- Appropriate pre-entry guidance
- Appropriate continuing guidance available
- Careers guidance readily available
- Accessible student welfare and counselling

Learning resources
- Well-stocked library and resource centre
- Open access to learning resources
- Open-access computer facilities available

Social and refreshment
- Affordable canteen facilities available when students require them
- Adequate sports facilities available
- Relaxation facilities available
- Opportunities for students to organize their own activities

Leadership

Head/Principal
- Head/Principal has vision and shares it
- Head/Principal walks the job
- Head/Principal knows the staff

	1	2	3	4	5

- Head/Principal knows the students
- Head/Principal provides leadership
- Head/Principal gives quality top priority

Values
- Mission clear and understood
- Equal opportunities policy in place and implemented
- Staff and students understand the college ethos
- Strong commitment to the needs of the community

Physical environment and resources

Buildings, classrooms and workshops
- Clean and attractive
- Fit for purpose
- Contain appropriate visual and learning aids

Stimulating learning environment
- Classroom layouts/individual learning programmes exciting to students
- Learning environments well planned and organized

Health and safety
- Student perception/incident logs kept
- Health and safety policies regularly monitored

Resource control and allocation
- Effective resource control exercised
- Resources controlled by those who use them

	1	2	3	4	5

Effective learning

Appropriateness of learning methods
- Teaching and learning strategies appropriate to the outcomes of the programmes
- Variety of learning modes available
- Teaching and learning strategies regularly reviewed and measured by a range of objective criteria
- Teaching and learning strategies measured by student response
- Learning is student-centred
- Students encouraged to take responsibility for their own learning
- Recognition of prior learning
- Evaluation methods used to gain customer responses
- Good climate of purposefulness amongst students

Appropriateness of the portfolio of courses
- Portfolio appropriate to learners' needs
- Content of programmes relevant and up to date
- Short response time to the development of new programmes
- Evaluation by clients of the relevance of the offering
- Good liaison with employers and the community on the delivery of programmes

Monitoring and evaluation
- Student feedback regularly obtained
- Feedback from other customer groups regularly obtained
- Student and community questionnaires used where appropriate

142

	1	2	3	4	5

- Institution has formal systems for review and evaluation
- Feedback used in policy-making

Students

Students matter
- Clear signs
- Clean and well-maintained toilets
- Student handbooks and guides available
- Staff talk to students
- Absence of artificial barriers
- Wide range of student services
- Good transport arrangements
- Range of leisure, recreation and sporting facilities available

Student satisfaction
- Good rapport between staff and students
- Happy students and satisfied customers evidenced through surveys and questionnaires
- Students have a sense of pride in their work
- Students kept informed
- Students' views regularly solicited

Staff

Attitude and motivation
- Committed and knowledgeable
- Student-centred
- Take responsibility for their own quality
- Have a sense of pride in their work
- Have a sense of enjoyment
- Respond readily to individual needs

	1	2	3	4	5

Teamwork
- Committed to teamwork and team approaches
- Have been trained in the skills of teamwork
- Have strong cohesion
- Have a clear idea of the limits to their authority
- Have a resource base that allows them to improve quality
- Value and support good practice
- Regularly consulted on policy

Staff development
- Institution committed to developing its staff
- Is proactive and clearly states institutional needs
- Has a review of individual needs
- Is adequately resourced and funded
- Is an institutional priority
- Includes all staff
- Positive staff development for TQM

Facilities
- Good workrooms
- Adequate and appropriate equipment and facilities
- Opportunities for professional discussion and debate

External relations

Marketing
- Coherent marketing strategy
- Market research and intelligence carried out
- Positive seeking out of customer views
- Student and employer questionnaires employed

	1	2	3	4	5

Community
- Excellent links with relevant communities maintained
- Community views regularly solicited
- Strong links with education/business partnerships

Organization

Strategic planning
- Institution has broad aims and objectives
- Staff at all levels are aware of the direction
- Institution has a written strategic plan
- Plan identifies how staff can contribute to success

Organizational culture
- Simple and lean structure
- Authority delegated down
- Change is part of the culture
- Universal statement of direction
- Strong commitment to peer evaluation and review
- Based on teamwork

Communications
- Good communication seen as major priority
- Bottom-up, not just top down
- Seen as the lifeblood of the institution

Standards

Hard standards
- Excellent exam results and student successes
- High progression rates into FE/HE/ employment
- Effective use of resources

	1	2	3	4	5

- Good student and community feedback based on systematic data collection
- Effective budgetary control

Soft standards
- Caring atmosphere
- Student welfare a priority
- Customer service in evidence
- Welcoming environment
- Commitment to learners of all abilities

Correct application of standards
- Institution does not measure itself on hard priorities alone

Bibliography

General

Albretcht, Karl (1988) *At America's Service*, Homewood, Illinios, Dow Jones-Irwin.

Artzt, Edwin L (1992) Welcome and Introductory Remarks, in Proctor & Gamble Company *The Total Quality Forum: Forging Strategic Links with Higher Education*, Report of the Proceedings August 1991, Cincinnati, Ohio, Proctor and Gamble.

Artzt, Edwin L, Burdick, W, Pipp, F, Robinson, J, Trotman, A, Pepper, J, (1992) 'Industry Executive Panel' in Proctor & Gamble Company *The Total Quality Forum: Forging Strategic Links with Higher Education*, Report of the Proceedings August 1991, Cincinnati, Ohio, Proctor and Gamble.

British Standards Institution (1987) *Quality Systems*, Parts 1–3; Part 4 1990, London, BSI.

British Standards Institution (February 1991) *BS5750 Guidance Notes For Application To Education and Training*, Milton Keynes, BSI.

British Standards Institution (May 1991) *Draft British Standard Guide to Total Quality Management*, BS7850, Part 1 Management, Part 2 Quality Improvement, Ref 91/89400 and 91/89401 London, BSI.

Christopher, Martin, Payne, Adrian and Ballantyne, David (1991) *Relationship Marketing*, Oxford, Butterworth Heinemann.

Crosby, Philip B (1979) *Quality Is Free*, New York, Mentor Books.

Deming, W Edwards (1986) *Out of the Crisis*, Cambridge, Cambridge University Press.

Department of Employment (1991) *Investors in People*, Sheffield, DoE.

Further Education Unit (1989) *Towards an Educational Audit*, London, FEU.

Haywood-Farmer, J (1990) 'A conceptual model of service quality' in Clarke, Graham, ed, *Managing Service Quality*, Bedford, IFS Publications.

Ishikawa, Kaoru (1985) *What Is Total Quality Control?* New Jersey, Prentice-Hall.

Juran, J M (1989) *Juran on Leadership for Quality*, New York, Macmillan.

Juran, J M and Gryna, Frank M, eds (1988) *Juran's Quality Control Handbook*, 4th edition, New York, McGraw-Hill.

Lascelles, D M and Dale, B G (1992) 'Quality improvement: the motivation and means of starting the process' in Hand, Max and Plowman, Brian, eds, *Quality Management Handbook*, Oxford, Butterworth Heinemann.

Macdonald, John and Piggott, John (1990) *Global Quality*, London, Mercury.

Malcolm Baldridge National Quality Award, 1991 Application Guidelines Washington DC, Department of Commerce, National Institute of Standards and Technology.

Mito, Setsuo (1990) *The Honda Book of Management*, London, Kogan Page

Oakland, John S (1989) *Total Quality Management*, Oxford, Heinemann.

PA Consulting Group (n.d.) *How to Take Part in the Quality Revolution: A Management Guide*, London, PA Consulting.

Peters, Tom (1987) *Thriving On Chaos*, London, Pan Books.

Peters, Tom and Austin, Nancy (1985) *A Passion for Excellence*, Glasgow, Fontana/Collins.

Peters, Tom and Waterman, Robert (1982) *In Search of Excellence*, New York, Harper and Row.

Pfeffer, Naomi and Coote, Anna (1991) *Is Quality Good for You?*, London, Social Policy Paper No 5, Institute of Public Policy Research.

Pirsig, Robert M (1974) *Zen And The Art Of Motorcylce Maintenance*, London, Vintage.

Rosander, A C (1989) *The Quest for Quality in Services*, Milwaukee, Wisconsin, Quality Press American Society for Quality Control.

Scholtes, Peter R et al (1988) *The Team Handbook*, Madison, Wisconsin, Joiner Associates Inc.

Tuckman, B W (1965) 'Development Sequences in Small Groups', *Psychological Bulletin*, Vol 63.

Unterberger, Robert M (July 1991) 'Quality is the Key to Global Competitiveness: IBM's Experience', in Petak, William J, ed, *Quality and Higher Education in the 21st Century*, Proceedings of the Second Annual Symposium: Role of Academia in National Competitiveness and Total Quality Management, University of Southern California Los Angeles.

van der Wiele, T, Snoep, P, Bertsch, J, Timmers, J, Williams, A R T, and Dale, B G (1990), 'Total Quality Management training and research in Europe : a state of the art survey' in Dale, B G and Williams, A R T, eds, *Education Training and Research in Total Quality Management*, Proceedings of the 1st European Conference, April 1990, Bedford, IFS Publications.

Walton, Mary (1986) *The Deming Management Method*, New York, Perigee Books.

Westley, Frances and Mintzberg, Henry (1991) 'Visionary leadership and strategic management' in Henry, Jane and Walker, David, eds, *Managing Innovation*, London, Open University and Sage Publications.

TQM in education

Atkinson, Tim (April 1990) *Evaluating Quality Circles in a College of Further Education*, Manchester Monographs, University of Manchester.

Elton, Lewis and Partington, Patricia (October 1991) *Teaching Standards and Excellence in Higher Education*, Occasional Green Paper No 1, Sheffield, Committee of Vice-Chancellors and Principals of the Universities of the United Kingdom.

Fox Valley Technical College (1991, 2nd edn) *Quality First Process Model*, Appleton, Wisconsin, The Academy for Quality in Education, Fox Valley Technical College Foundation.

Gray, Lynton, Foreword to Sallis, Edward and Hingley, Peter (1992) *Total Quality Management*, Coombe Lodge Report, Volume 13, No 1, Blagdon, The Staff College.

HMI (Summer 1991) *Quality Assurance in Colleges of Further Education*, Reference 92/92/NS, London, Department of Education and Science.

Kaplan, Robert, (1992) Keynote Address in Proctor and Gamble Company *The Total Quality Forum: Forging Strategic Links with Higher Education*, Report of the Proceedings August 1991, Cincinnati, Ohio, Proctor and Gamble.

Miller, John, Dower, Allison and Inniss, Sonia (1989, 1992) *Improving Quality in Further Education: A Guide for Teachers in Course Teams*, Ware, Herts, Consultants at Work.

Miller, John and Inniss, Sonia (1990) *Managing Quality Improvement in Further Education: A Guide for Middle Managers*, Ware, Herts.

Miller, John and Inniss, Sonia (1992) *Strategic Quality Management*, Ware, Herts.

Pardy, David (January 1992) *Quality Assurance*, Conference Paper CP516, Blagdon, The Staff College.

Petak, William J, ed (July 1991) *Quality and Higher Education*, Proceedings of the Second Annual Symposium, Role of Academia in National Competitiveness and Total Quality Management, University of Southern California Los Angeles.

Proctor & Gamble Company (1992) *The Total Quality Forum: Forging Strategic Links with Higher Education*, Report of the Proceedings August 1991 Cincinnati, Ohio, Proctor and Gamble.

Roberts, A (1992) *Establishing Customer Needs and Perceptions*, Mendip Paper MP 031, Blagdon, The Staff College.

Ruston, Rod (1992) 'BS5750 in Educational Establishments' in Sallis, Edward and Hingley, Peter, *Total Quality Management*, Coombe Lodge Report Vol 23, No 1, Blagdon, The Staff College.

Sallis, Edward (1990) 'Corporate Planning in an FE College', *Educational Management and Administration*, Vol 18, No 2.

Sallis, Edward (Spring 1990) 'The Evaluation of Quality in Further Education', *Education Today*, Vol 40, No 2.

Sallis, Edward (1991) *The National Quality Survey*, Mendip Paper MP 009, Blagdon, The Staff College.

Sallis, Edward (1992) 'Total Quality Management and standards in further education' in Harry Tomlinson, ed., *The Search for Standards*, Harlow, Longman.

Sallis, Edward and Hingley, Peter (1991) *College Quality Assurance Systems*, Mendip Paper MP 020, Blagdon, The Staff College.

Sallis, Edward, Hingley, Peter and other contributors (1992) *Total Quality Management*, Coombe Lodge Report, Vol 23, No 1, Blagdon, The Staff College.

Spanbauer, Stanley J (1987) *Quality First in Education ... Why Not?*, Appleton, Wisconsin, Fox Valley Technical College Foundation.

Spanbauer, Stanley J (1989) *Measuring and Costing Quality in Education*, Appleton, Wisconsin, Fox Valley Technical College Foundation.

Spanbauer, Stanley J (1992) *A Quality System For Education*, Milwaukee, Wisconsin, ASQC Quality Press.

Tansley, Paula (1989) *Course Teams – The Way Forward in FE?* Windsor, NFER-Nelson.

Training Enterprise and Education Directorate of the Department of Employment (November 1990) *The Management of Quality: BS5750 and Beyond*, Sheffield, Training Quality Branch, Training Enterprise and Education, Directorate Employment Department Group.

Index

Other Books on Quality from Kogan Page

How to Design and Deliver Quality Service Training
Tony Newby
ISBN 0 7494 0737 9

Training for Total Quality Management
Bill Evans, Peter Reynolds and Dave Jeffries
ISBN 0 7494 0754 9

Total Quality
A Manager's Guide for the 1990s
The Ernst and Young Quality Improvement Consulting Group
ISBN 0 7494 0864 2

Total Quality Marketing
What Has To Come Next in Sales, Marketing and Advertising
John Fraser-Robinson
ISBN 0 7494 0389 6

Quality at Work
Diane Bone and Rick Griggs
HB ISBN 0 7494 0033 1
PB ISBN 0 7494 0034 X

The Quality Movement
Helga Drummond
ISBN 0 7494 0753 0

The Quality Manual
How to Write and Develop a Successful Manual for Quality
Management Systems
Jenny Waller, Derek Allen and Andy Burns
ISBN 0 7494 0903 7

Quality Assurance in Training and Education
How to Apply BS5750 (ISO9000) Standards
Richard Freeman
ISBN 0 7494 0868 5

Quality Assurance and Accountability in Higher Education
Edited by Cari P Loder
ISBN 1 85091 888 0

Quality in Learning
A Capability Approach in Higher Education
Edited by John Stephenson and Susan Weil
ISBN 0 7494 0699 2